Speak to Me That I May Speak

Speak to Me That I May Speak

A Spirituality of Preaching

W. Dow Edgerton

THE
PILGRIM
PRESS
Cleveland

Acknowledgment is gratefully given for permission to quote from the following:

"Transcendental Etude," from *The Dream of a Common Language: Poems 1974–1977* by Adrienne Rich. Copyright © 1978 by W. W. Norton & Company, Inc. Used by permission of the author and W. W. Norton & Company, Inc.

"The Ninth Elegy," copyright © 1982 by Stephen Mitchell, from *The Selected Poetry of Rainer Maria Rilke* by Rainer Maria Rilke, translated by Stephen Mitchell. Used by permission of Random House, Inc.

"Notes Toward a Poem That Can Never Be Written," from *Selected Poems II: Poems Selected and New*. Copyright © 1987 by Margaret Atwood. Reprinted by permission of Houghton Mifflin Company. All rights reserved.

"The Way In" from *Selected Poems of Rainer Maria Rilke, A Translation from the German and Commentary by Robert Bly*. Copyright © 1981 by Robert Bly. Reprinted by permission of Harper Collins Publishers.

The Pilgrim Press
700 Prospect Avenue
Cleveland, Ohio 44115-1100
thepilgrimpress.com

Printed in the United States of America on acid-free paper

11 10 09 08 07 06   5 4 3 2 1

Library of Congress Cataloging-in-Publication Data

Edgerton, W. Dow, 1948-
    Speak to me that I may speak : a spirituality of preaching / W. Dow
Edgerton.
        p. cm.
    ISBN 0-8298-1719-0
    1. Preaching. 2. Clergy – Religious life. I. Title.
BV4211.3.E34 2006
251 – dc22

                                                    2005028968

ISBN-13: 978-0-8298-1719-5
ISBN-10: 0-8298-1719-0

Contents

Preface

Think of the situation of a preacher who is once again preparing to preach. Think about a preacher who, for whatever reason (perhaps the grace of God!), hesitates. Before the book is opened, before there is a mark on the page, before there is a text in which to lose oneself, before all the composing and arranging of thoughts, words, and images, this preacher hesitates and asks, "What is it I am preparing to do?"

This is a book about the extraordinary task that lies at the heart of the preaching ministry. It grows from the conviction that the work of interpretation, reflection, and preparing to preach is at the core of the preacher's spiritual life and deserves our ever deeper attention. It grows from the conviction that this daily work, so well known and accustomed, is nevertheless a process by which the preacher's own life and faith are transformed. "Morning by morning God wakens — wakens my ear to listen as those who are taught" (Isa. 50:4), says the prophet. As the old hymn prays, "Lord, speak to me that I may speak."

One

In the Beginning

It begins in the morning ◆ The tongue of one who is taught ◆
Method and discipline ◆ The spiritual ◆ Spiritual discipline ◆
In the beginning — Brooding over the face of the deep ◆ The
contradiction of contradiction ◆ Knowledge ◆ Fortitude ◆ The
counsel of mercy ◆ Love of the enemy ◆ Wisdom

It begins in the morning

I respond *although* I will be changed.

— Eugen Rosenstock-Huessy[1]

It begins in the morning, when the day begins. The dreams have
ended again, for now. What you have seen and heard and felt
has already begun to fade. There are some details that stick in
your mind, however. Lying in bed, without your even intend-
ing it, questions float forward about the reason for those faces
and rooms, that street, that song. "Where is that stream, and
why did I dream about it?" The day begins with another un-
readable dream fading while the definite tasks of the hours ahead
reassemble themselves.

So a prayer upon rising:

Blessed art thou, O God, Creator of the Universe, for you
raise up those who are bowed down.

Pray a prayer for the eyes by which you hope to see:

> Blessed art thou, O God, Creator of the Universe, for you open the eyes of those who are blind.

Pray a prayer for the ears by which you hope to hear:

> Blessed art thou, O God, Creator of the Universe, for you open the ears of those who are deaf.

What necessary blessings for someone whose day will be lived trying to understand what the ears are hearing and the eyes are seeing!

The face in the mirror, the faces at the table, the faces in the morning paper. Talk of school, of schedules, of lunches; talk of weather, scores, traffic; comfortable assurances of love, reassuring ceremonies of departure: it all has meaning. Some of it a person knows well enough and can explain, and some of it is as puzzling as last night's dream.

A morning in ordinary time. You arrive at the church, turn up the heat in the study. Then you wonder about the fuel bill, turn it back a little, and take the spare sweater out of the closet. The building is quiet. You open the Bible and begin reading the texts for the coming Sunday. Last week is finished and the preparation has to begin all over again. All over again from the beginning, the reading, the study, the musing, the reverie, the search through experience and memory, half looking for ideas, half trying to get rid of them, the search for that certain poem hidden somewhere on the shelf among the thousands of pages there is no time to read.

All over again begins the search for words, images, connections. But also the search for something else: compassion, spirit, soul, "matteredness."

In a few days' time little at all may have happened. The texts may remain closed in upon themselves, and you closed in the same way, with no bridge built on which to pass back and forth.

The time will come to preach and there will be nothing to do but repeat in faith, hope, and humility what you have already said on other occasions.

That is not necessarily a bad thing. Sometimes that is the very best, and the most that one is called to do.

In a few days' time, however, you may well have changed. That's often what happens to a person who does this kind of work. The Bible talks about a two-edged sword dividing soul from spirit, joints from marrow, judging the contents of the heart. It has happened before, after all, that words on the page required much of you to allow you to preach them, not just repeat them. It is true because much is required of those who are given much; much is required, *because* so much is given. That may be the more alarming truth about this journey which begins again today: not that so much will be required of you in order to preach, but that so much may be given to you that preaching will be the slimmest gesture of response.

The pages in front of you may, in the days ahead, bring you to conviction, to confession, to repentance, to peace-making with enemies you don't want to make peace with, to promises, to quite real risk, to decision, to costly commitment, to joy, that is to say, of the sort Jesus talked about when he said, "Blessed are. . . . " Any of this may be what lies ahead, opening the Book on a morning in ordinary time.

The tongue of one who is taught

The Lord GOD has given me
   the tongue of one who is taught,
That I may know how to sustain
   the weary with a word.
Morning by morning [God] wakens —
   wakens my ear
     to listen as those who are taught.

The Lord GOD has opened my ear,
   and I was not rebellious,
   I did not turn backward.
I gave my cheeks to those who pulled out the beard;
I did not hide my face
   from insult and spitting.

The Lord GOD helps me;
   therefore I have not been disgraced;
   therefore I have set my face like flint,
   and I know that I shall not be put to shame;
   [the one] who vindicates me is near.
Who will contend with me?
   Let us stand up together.
Who are my adversaries?
   Let them confront me.
It is the Lord GOD who helps me,
   who will declare me guilty?
All of them will wear out like a garment;
   the moth will eat them up.

Who among you fears the LORD
   And obeys the voice of [God's] servant,
who walks in darkness and has no light,
yet trusts in the name of the LORD,
   and relies upon [the Servant's] God?
But all of you are kindlers of fire,
   lighters of firebrands.
Walk in the flame of your fire,
   and among the brands that you have kindled!

—Isaiah 50:4–10 NRSV adapted

So sings the Servant in the words of the prophet Isaiah. The
Servant is given an ability to speak that comes from hearing. And
this ability is for the sake of the weary who can be sustained by

a word. I don't know which is more marvelous: that one could speak as someone who truly listened, or that a weary person could be sustained by a word. Maybe they are the same marvel, different aspects of the same truth.

I hope a sustaining word can, indeed, be spoken by those — by you — who have received a gift of listening. Strange gift: a gift of receiving, of openness. A gift of no gift, but the power to respond. It sounds like a kind of promise, that there will be something to be heard. Why else give a gift of listening if there is nothing to be heard? Yet the Servant Song doesn't say who will teach. Perhaps it is God who will teach, perhaps it is the weary themselves who will teach. The text tells not of the teacher, but only of the taught.

I hope a sustaining word can, indeed, be heard by the weary in my congregation, in yours or wherever else they may be — something that makes all the difference. Strange gift: only a word, maybe not such an impressive word, at that. There is part of me, I confess, that wants to read a different word there. Healing, let's say, or freeing, saving — some more important and final-sounding word. But there is reality and wisdom to the more modest term. A word to sustain the weary is really a marvelous thing. To share strength, the power to continue in the face of what erodes, drains the ability to live, a word that holds someone despite the aimed heart-blows that would suck the air out of them — this would be much help, indeed. I want to know how a word can sustain the weary. I want to learn how to listen as those who are taught.

"Come to me all you who labor and are heavy laden, and I will give you rest," Jesus says. "For my yoke is easy, and my burden is light." Jesus promises rest and more, a great paradox: an easy yoke and a light burden. How can that be? "Is not this the fast that I choose: to loose the bonds of injustice, to undo the thongs of the yoke, to let the oppressed go free, and to break every yoke?" (Isa. 58:6). I should think a yoke is precisely what cannot be easy, no matter how comfortable, simply because it is a yoke. I should think a burden is burdensome, and heavy, regardless of its weight, simply because it is a burden. Yet somehow Jesus promises a rest despite the reality of burden, and freedom even before all the yokes are broken. I want to know how a yoke can be easy and a burden light. I want to know how a word can do such a thing as sustain the weary. I want to learn how to listen as those who are taught.

And because the Servant sustains with only a word those who are weary, there is now the enmity of the *weariers* to contend with, whether they are flesh and blood or principalities and powers. Why would this be? Is it somehow different to sustain with a word than with a cup of cold water or a piece of bread? Is it somehow more dangerous to the weariers? Exactly so. A cup of cold water is good and necessary and must be given if one has the power. Bread is good and necessary and must be given if one has the power. But not a cup of cold water and silence, not bread and silence.

To sustain those who are weary with a word means to sustain by telling the truth. The Servant whose ear is awakened by the God who also hears — and answers — the cry of the weary: such a person is dangerous to the weariers. They may control the price of cold water and bread, make the supply small and the demand great. But with the truth it is a different economy. The greater the need, the more is given. "Ho, everyone who thirsts, come to the waters; and you that have no money, come, buy and eat!" (Isa. 55:1), says the prophet. I want to know how a word can do such a thing as sustain the weary. I want to learn how to listen as those who are taught.

If you are the Servant, however, there is a cost: the exposure of your own face. How can you speak to the weary if your face is hidden? How can you invite another to lift up his or her face that it may shine if you lower your own? How can you sustain them without turning toward them — in the café, in the street, in the hospital, in the sanctuary — and facing beyond and behind them, those whose shape casts its pall, blocks out the light? This is the cost of listening, just of listening with a God-opened ear, as one who is taught. An unhidden face, exposed, vulnerable to humiliation. You look in the mirror and see your own face set like flint, not a welcome thing to see. Not the face you wanted for your face, hard like that. Nevertheless, I want to know how a word can sustain the weary. I want to learn how to listen as those who are taught.

Will there be help? The Servant says there has been already, and is, and will be. There is contention and confrontation, yes. There are adversaries of the most serious kind, yes. There are accusers, yes, who do their work well, whether openly or from hiding. But the weariers one can see cannot overcome the near and unseen God who takes away shame and disgrace, who gives vindication, who stands with those who are accused for the sin of opening their ears to listen as one who is taught for the sake of the weary.

Yet despite help and nearness, the Servant must walk in darkness and without light, without seeing, without certainty, and without the presence. The Servant must walk with a word and the Name. Trusting in the Name, finally unutterable except by God, trusting in a Name that one cannot say. Yet it is a Name, nonetheless, a Name one can *hear,* hear like a promise, hear in the dark, where truth makes the darkness shine brighter than light.

Who, indeed, would listen to such a servant? Who would leave behind the false assurance of false light to walk in the darkness of the unseen God for whom darkness is light, and light is darkness? Who would leave behind the land of false light to walk where the unseen God is to be heard and trusted? Or rather, who would exchange such a luminous and echoing darkness for the small lights of the weariers, flickering lights, little fires that dazzle your eyes only when they are held close to your face? The weariers can't answer this. The weariers love their own light because they have made it, because it narrows the dark of the their eyes. Who would listen to such a servant? The weariers can't answer. But the weary can. So I want to know how a word can sustain the weary, and I want to hear a word that can sustain the weary. I want to learn how to listen as those who are taught.

Method and discipline

Method. Method has to do with a road, not the *map* of a road, but the road itself. The map is not the territory, as the saying goes. Neither is territory a walk *in* territory. To speak of method is to speak of a way; to speak of a way is to speak of a walk; to speak of a walk which is a way of living is to speak of a practice; to speak of a practice upon which one reflects and which transforms us is to speak of a praxis. To take such a praxis, finally, and bind oneself to it — by covenant, by a promise, by a vow: this is freedom. To claim this freedom anew day after day: this is a discipline. Each transformation by which method moves toward discipline is a step more deeply into commitment. This is another way of saying a step toward truth of an existential kind.

For those who must interpret in order to speak, interpretation is a way of life. Whether or not it is a discipline is a different question. To say it is a way of life means that the day, the week, the season, the year, the path of a lifetime all are framed by the demands and freedoms of the process of interpretation. The path of interpretation becomes the story of the day. The story of the day finds its place in the story of the week, the year, the season, the lifetime, the age. If interpretation is to become a discipline it must become more than one's schedule and situation — an external set of demands to be fulfilled, the exigencies of the job. If it is to become a discipline it must be a transformative praxis to which you bind yourself.

But let us also use another word with a different sense: cadence. Discipline is the cadence, the rhythm of interpretive life. When I hear the word "discipline," let me hear the drum, "a timbrel...which musicians strike in a measured, disciplined way..." (Cassiodorus, Ps. 150:4).[2] And if it is a rhythm, then it is an embodied rhythm, made with the body and the complexity of beat of which even the single body is capable — and indeed, which can only be realized by the body in dialogue with itself: the fingers, the palm of the hand, the feet, shoulders, head, hips, mouth. You carry the rhythm that carries you. This, too, is a discipline.

In ancient eucharistic theology the logic of transformation was the logic of becoming what you eat. We eat bread and become bread. The transformation is mutual, the bread into the eater, the eater into the bread. So with this work of interpretation: the praxis of interpretation becomes the story of your life, and the story of your life becomes the praxis of your interpretation. I am the person who has interpreted *this* way. Who I shall be depends upon the interpretation that unfolds from here and how it is connected to the ever larger story in which meaning is framed.

A photographer or painter will make a small window by bending a forefinger at a right angle to the thumb. Hold it out at arm's length and the focus is very tight: the arm of a chair, the handle of the door, the vane on the roof. Bring it closer to your eye and you see the corner of the study with the bookshelves, the street beyond the open door, the cloud front moving in from the west. Bring it closer and the frame becomes larger still until you can't see the frame itself and the only limit to what you can see is the limit of your own sight.

A verse becomes a page, a page becomes a book. A moment becomes a day, a day becomes a year, a life. A glance becomes a conversation, a conversation becomes a friendship, a love. A pang of loss becomes sadness, sadness becomes a grief, grief becomes a mourning for all that has ever been lost. A smile becomes a laugh, a laugh becomes joy, joy becomes endless praise — and endless praise becomes, once again, a verse.

The spiritual

The word "spiritual" itself must give us pause. Like the word "love" it has been used for the most contradictory purposes, its meaning bound to terrible and wonderful histories.

For some the word is immediately appealing. It suggests dimensions of holiness, mystery, depth; it belongs to transcendence, the beyond, ultimate things. The word draws together the desire for what is beautiful, true, and good. "Spiritual" points toward things invisible but real, ineffable but present, unutterable but perceivable, if not by ordinary means, then by a special hearing, sight, or sense.

For some the word is immediately appalling. It belongs to the retreat from the body, the earth, the common human world — and from whoever or whatever is associated with body, earth, and common humanity. "Spiritual" points away from realities and demands for action, away from responsibility in the world. It establishes a hidden realm with hidden powers, powers with authority that can't be questioned or called to account, arbitrary, mystified, veiled in arcane jargon — to the particular benefit of those who do the veiling. The "spiritual" means special pleading, avoidance of the claims of reason, avoidance of lived experience, actual conditions, and practical wisdom.

It is not only "despisers of religion" who have held this view, nor simply those who hold to some crass and mechanical materialism. The prophets of the Bible powerfully resisted the spiritualization of the God who hates the noise of solemn assemblies while there is no one to give justice in the gates. Bring justice and mercy, they insisted, not incense and offerings.

By the same token, however, it has often been those accused of otherworldliness and fantastic thinking who have borne witness most powerfully to a transcendent claim of justice and mercy. It is they who have sustained the weary with a word. When the world falls prey to the power of death, from where does the strength to speak a word of life come? For some the "spiritual" has provided an open place in which to imagine life shaped differently, free from the principalities and powers that dominate body, mind, earth, and human affairs. From this open place have come vital visions of the dignity and holiness of body, mind, earth, and community.

The word "spiritual" means all of what has just been said, and more — and sometimes less, for that matter. Of its own "spiritual" is no better or worse than some other word, no more worthy of our respect or fear. But it demands of us a special responsibility to say what we mean.

"Spiritual" is often used in two different senses. One sense refers to a region or dimension of the world (or beyond it). To speak of spiritual things in this sense means to refer to realities in which we live and move and have our being, the great visible and invisible, audible and inaudible mystery. A second sense of "spiritual" refers to a concern, an orientation, an awareness. To speak of spiritual things in this sense means to speak of a person or a community's way of understanding and living its life in the world. I intend the word in each of these senses (in particular ways), and both of them together.

As to the first of these senses: "spiritual" here does not refer to a special realm or region, whether in the world or beyond it; it refers, rather, to what is always already *at hand* in its difficulty, complexity, and "matteredness." What is at hand is never simple and single. It is part of a web of relations: people, things, places, events, histories, texts, images, language — especially language. Confessionally, I would speak of God, world, and humankind. It is in this web of relations that things are what they are, neither dissolving into one another nor standing free of one another. By "spiritual" I refer to this relationality, the *in-between,* the space where the meeting happens by which God, world, and humankind are what they are.

What kind of space is this? It is in this space that call and response occur. From one side may come command, name, plea, invitation, curse, blessing, silence, forgiveness, promise. From another may come prayer, lament, hymn, obedience, rejection, disobedience, demand, thanksgiving, vow. From another may come texts of story, psalm, law, vision, letter, prophecy, wisdom, philosophy. From another may come roar, cry, rustle, splash, howl, song. From another may come seed, shoot, root, branch, flower, fruit. From yet another may come swirls and currents, the heave of mountains, the lights in the sky.

None of them by themselves are the spiritual, or closer or farther away of themselves.

The spiritual is the between space around which they meet, through which they disclose themselves to one another and themselves, by virtue of which they hear, and by the power of which each answers in its particular speech.

As to the second of these senses: spiritual here refers to the concern for what is *at stake* in the meeting at hand. It means a kind of attentiveness, an intentionality, dwelling in what is always already at stake and at hand, returning to its difficulty not as a place where matters are resolved but where they are revealed.

Spirituality in this sense, is *attending. Ad-tendere,* to reach toward. It's a good, physical word. Attend, attending, attention. It can mean to be present, to see to or carry out, to wait upon, to focus one's mind, to stand ready to act, to care for. Spirituality means attending to the *in-between* on each (or every) side of which stand the questioner and the questioned. If we understand *attention* in this rich way, we can say simply spirituality is attending to what is at stake between us at the intersection of God, world, and persons — listening with the ear of one who is taught.

This is why one must speak of spiritual *discipline.* Discipline points to the character and quality of our attention. It emphasizes that spirituality has everything to do with hours, days, weeks, and years. It confesses there is something in me that does not *want* to attend to the in-between, to questions, to the difficult. It recognizes there is something in me that seeks to remake the spiritual into clouds and mist. *Discipline* confesses the powerful temptation to transform spirituality into its opposite, a transformation which happens so silently and invisibly that one is unaware that anything has changed.

How can we tell when spirituality has been inverted in such a way? It has to do with what the Hebrew Bible calls *mishpat,* or right-relation, justice. If we understand that spirituality is attending to the in-between of God, world, and persons, and if we understand that attending includes presence, care, and response, then acting to establish or restore right relation is the goal of spiritual life. This is the *discipline.* This is the following through by which our attention becomes (at last) spiritual.

To speak of discipline is not to add something to the spiritual as if the spiritual could be spiritual by itself. It is, indeed, more accustomed for me to suppose that I know what the words "spiritual" and "discipline" mean quite apart from each other, and have only to bring them together to modify one another in order to understand their combination. It is a much different thing to suppose that I do *not* know them apart from each other, and I can come to know them only as they meet. *Spiritual* and *discipline* reveal themselves to one another and through one another. The farther they are separated from one another, the more each one fades in intensity, the less itself it becomes until the distance is so great each is left as a bare cipher: letters on a page, sounds in the air, but crucially emptied of meaning. Together they are not one another's antithesis, but one another's realization.

Let us say it even more strongly. Just as *spiritual* and *discipline* become what they are through their encounter, *I,* too, am realized in the same way. I am who I am because of the words that meet and reveal themselves in and because of my presence, and by which in the presence of which, I am revealed. You read a passage of scripture and the words that make you who you are respond and begin to echo inside — memory, hope, fear, faith. The words inside begin to sound and your voice discloses who you are, not only to others, but also to you.

Spiritual discipline

If you were to trace the way the term "spiritual discipline" has been used you would probably find much what you'd expect, with perhaps a few surprises. You would find elements of pattern and repetition, of rule, of ordinary tasks and times somehow transformed (or confirmed so deeply as to have one's view of them transformed). You would find elements of what some traditions call prayer. You would find elements of what some traditions call contemplation. Often you would find a dimension of discipleship following a Teaching, sometimes a Teacher.

You would also find what has been called "mysticism," a word that may be fascinating, irritating, or repellent (perhaps all to the same person). Writing as a historian, Bernard McGinn observed "mysticism is primarily (not solely) an ecclesial tradition of prayer and practice nourished by scripture and liturgy, in order to foster awareness of whatever direct forms of divine presence may be available in this life."[3] There is a disarming directness and modesty to much of the description, perhaps even ordinariness. There is a dimension of receiving and handing on (*traditio*), a dimension of community or communion, a joining of the inward and the outward, sacred texts and a rhythm shaped through ritual practice (in general) or a liturgy (in particular).

Some of this may be surprising if one's image of mysticism has emphasized elements of the extraordinary, the singular, the ecstatic. Indeed, those may be the very elements that draw a person onto a mystical path, and they may be the aspects of spiritual life that most command the attention of searchers. What is frequently overlooked, however, are the ordinary realities of which the path actually consists. Whatever the experiences are that may be called mystical, they are held within a surprisingly (perhaps) mundane tracery of life, its threads spun of community, scripture, and worship.

The descriptive part is straightforward enough, so straightforward as to lull one into reading too quickly what comes next. Why does a person undertake such practices? "...In order to foster whatever direct forms of divine presence may be available in this life...." It is one thing to write or read as a historian describing the intentions and self-understanding of representatives of a tradition. It is another thing to write or read as a person seeking to understand what the goal of one's own practice is. It is another thing still to pause and wonder over such words as "whatever direct forms of divine presence might be available in this life."

Special poignancy attaches to a certain contrast in the words. There is, on one hand, a kind of audacity to speaking of "direct forms of divine presence." Moses was hid in the cleft of a rock lest God's glory destroy him upon the mountain. In the tent of meeting, the scriptures say, Moses and God spoke face to face as friends (Exod. 33). But that so charged Moses that his face had to be veiled because the shine on him frightened the people. Divine presence? Who should want the day of the Lord, a day of cloud and thick gloom, a day of winnowing, fires, melting, and remolding?

God spoke to Abraham and it became the most terrible of tests. Jeremiah raged that he had been despoiled by God, seduced, used, left to the ridicule of those around him. Is it necessary to speak of Jesus? Is it not for our sake that God hides? Isn't it a mercy?

So there is something audacious and even alarming to "direct forms of divine presence." The poignancy comes with the words that surround it: "whatever...might be possible in this life." Let us grant that no one shall see God and live. Let us grant that whether it is in unapproachable light or impenetrable dark, God hides for our own safety.

Then what is left? In the terms of the human life we know, what *is* possible? Of the presence God promised to Moses, or the accompaniment Jesus vowed to the disciples, of the indwelling spirit the evangelist John reports Jesus to have promised before his death — a presence to console them in his absence — *whatever is possible....* What is left?

Whatever such presence may be it will have to be met in a day pretty much like today: sometime between waking and sleeping, sometime between sitting down at the table and rising up, sometime between ordering coffee and paying the bill, sometime between hanging up the telephone and turning back to the desk, sometime between opening the Bible and closing it.

If yours is, indeed, a life of interpretation, then whatever presence is possible will have to be met in the practice of interpretation itself. Whatever presence there may be must be discerned there. And if what is available is only absence, what then? If one "walks in darkness and has no light, yet trusts in the name of the Lord," what then? Do we attend to the *absence* just as we attend to the presence? Do we bring the absence to bear upon what we are thinking and feeling, reading, writing, and saying? Surely this, too, is part of spiritual discipline, perhaps the greatest part, the part that *requires* discipline.

An old preacher once advised me, "Preach your faith, not your doubts." Fair enough, and good advice. But we have not yet come to preaching. And if faith is to be preached — from faith to faith — then we must interpret and preach from the very place where faith is distinctively what it is. In the question of presence and absence and what may be possible, faith is what holds open a place for presence where there is no presence. In the presence of the Presence what need is there of faith? Or what need of preaching, for that matter? In the Presence our speech will take care of itself and no one needs to say to another "know God" (Jer. 31). It is absence that faith as *faith* knows best. If faith is the substance of things unseen, then it lives from absence and is what it is precisely because it holds open the empty place, even guards the empty place, and refuses to let it be filled by what is not God.

First step: In the beginning—
Brooding over the face of the deep

Whatever else a beginning is, if it is really a beginning, it is a place of brooding over the face of the deep. If it is really a beginning it is a place of dividing and joining, distinguishing and naming, appearing, gathering, putting forth, yielding, bearing, setting, swarming, swimming, creeping, imaging, blessing.

At the beginning the most basic questions are open for discussion as real questions. The work is basic and radical, and therefore the basic questions are radical, or at least they seek responses that are. Having answered before is more hindrance than help. Having known once, or a thousand times, disguises the truth that to begin again is to be interrogated again and give account again. Why this Book? Why am I preaching? Why are they listening? What can these words possibly mean, and for whom? These are not abstract questions if you are the one who must read, understand, and speak. These are not questions someone else can answer for you, not even the *you* who has answered before. And if you *are* able to affirm once again today what you have affirmed in the past, let it be because you have discovered again today what you are to do. But who can return to basic questions each week when already the Book is open, and already there is too little time? And how can one *begin* with affirmation or confession when it is only through the interpretive path itself that you will discover a way to affirm or confess?

"Before all it is necessary . . . " wrote Augustine in *On Christian Doctrine* as he began to unfold a spirituality of interpretation. He described a kind of ladder or progression by which the interpreter of the scripture must be transformed. From fear of God to faith, from faith to knowledge, from knowledge to fortitude through a hunger and thirst for justice, from fortitude to the counsel of mercy, from the counsel of mercy to love of the enemy, and finally from the love of the enemy to wisdom. At the beginning the claim of transformation is already made. There is no fiction of "immaculate perception" on the part of the interpreter, but a recognition that interpretation itself *requires* transformation. Yet it is clear in Augustine's own writing that the work of interpretation is itself transformative. The beginning of interpretation requires transformation, and the transformation proceeds through the interpretation itself. The goal is the journey; the journey is the goal.

The particular path Augustine describes, of course, must be weighed carefully. His own transformation was incomplete, as he well knew. He, too, saw only puzzling reflections in a mirror. That makes his reflections all the more a gift, because we can think *with* him for a while with no requirement to think *like* him, and consider in our own terms how what he says could be understood, and understood differently.

"Before all it is necessary that we be turned by the fear of God toward a recognition of God's will" wrote Augustine.[4] What a hard place to start! Impossible for some, unreasonable for some, and for some simply wrong. Why fear as a starting place? Perhaps because we will start with fear whether we acknowledge it or not, because fear is so thoroughly woven into the fabric of our life, so intricately woven the thread can scarcely be singled out at times. In my own journey, the fear of God has been sometimes a source of suffering, sometimes the only thing that makes sense. Sometimes it has been stupid and senseless, sometimes the beginning of wisdom. I have heard the fear of God both dismissed and trumpeted, both for reasons equally thin. It is necessary, I believe, to speak of the fear of God, what it must *not* mean, and what it is *needed* to mean.

There is the kind of fear that is, indeed, *used* to threaten, frighten and control, the kind of fear directed against life. This is the kind of fear which, the church must confess, it has often employed. It is the quintessential mark of the abuser, and we must acknowledge that Christians have to an astonishing extent encouraged, allowed, or simply stood silent while the God of Abuse was set up as a desecrating sacrilege in the place of the gospel. It is all the more remarkable, when we consider how prominently the word of angels in the scriptures is "Fear not."

There is a kind of fear that is a fear of death, and those who have the power of death understand this fear very well. The power of death reaches into every aspect of life and distorts it. It reaches into every act, relationship, community, and perception. It becomes, we could say, a kind of *economy* as death circulates through all these aspects of our life. Paradoxically enough, this economy of death presents itself as the protector of life, our security. One flees to the power of death for shelter from the power of death.

This power reaches into every interpretation, as well, which should give one pause. This power of death claims a person so completely that it becomes invisible, and even worse. Not content to hold a person captive from without, it holds a person captive from within so that we do not see when we ourselves have become so convinced by death as to become its servants. It is present in the scriptures themselves. A hard thing to say and think, that the power of death is at work also in the scriptures, and the scriptures themselves may serve the fear of death rather than the fear of God. Some will object that it is not the scriptures that are deadly, only how they are used. Often that may indeed be the case. This, however, is finally a denial of the depth of the crisis that confronts us, perhaps in hope that there is somewhere inscribed some pure speech untainted by the fundamental contradiction of human life. This, of course, is the very denial by which the power of death conceals itself, appearing as its opposite. It is precisely where the claim of pure speech is held most strongly that the scriptures are used most violently: bondage masquerades as freedom; lawlessness masquerades as law. Who will deliver us from this body of death?

Yet the Psalmist writes of a different fear. "God takes pleasure in those who fear God, in those who hope in God's steadfast love" (Ps. 147:11). A strange way to speak of fear: fear as hope in God's steadfast love. Who is the God of whom the Psalmist sings there? The one who gathers outcasts, heals the brokenhearted, lifts up the downtrodden, casts down the wicked, sets creation in order, grants shalom, and who *speaks* to God's people. The one, Christians testify, who in Jesus came to "free those who all their lives were held in slavery by the fear of death" (Heb. 2:15).

The fear that serves the power of death itself is afraid of God. The fear by which I have come to be justly numbered among the wicked, this fear is afraid of God. The fear that the power of death works into the whole cloth of our life together — this fear is afraid of God. The fear which does not want to be cast out, which wants to hold us captive and remain hidden behind our eyes so we cannot see except with eyes of fear — this fear is afraid of God. So convinced by the power of death that I cannot imagine life beyond its power, I therefore must recognize this truth at the very beginning. I must recognize that the fear of God itself becomes distorted into its opposite, into a fear of death, and shaped into yet another expression of my bondage and terror (perhaps the most deceptive of all). The great deception is to suppose that by denying or turning from the fear of God I can evade the power of death when in truth all I evade is the truth of my captivity.

Interpretation that begins with the fear of God, therefore, begins in the recognition of how deeply contradicted and set against life — including my own — I can be. It begins with the recognition that death is afraid of its own death within me and among us, and that the fear of *God* (as something that makes us afraid) is the fear of life and freedom. It begins with this fundamental affirmation of the power of life and freedom, which necessarily means my own need for transformation. To begin with the fear of God is to begin with the reality of my fearful response to the threat of life as the starting point of interpretation.

The fear of God, however, is indeed the *starting point,* not the goal. Without recognizing my own deep contradiction, interpretation will remain within the safe (strange to say) economy of death. To follow Augustine's path, it must be led to a second next step, the step of piety or faith.

Second step:
The contradiction of contradiction

No preacher is stranger to contradiction. The morning mirror is reminder enough, and a moment's conversation with neighbor or passerby confirms that it is in us all. The sanctuary that is empty now will be full of contradiction come Sunday: contradiction within and without, in mind, body, spirit, relationship, and community. Ultimate struggles of life and death are played out in the unremarkable conversation between mother and daughter at breakfast, a man choosing coffee at the grocery store, and a child choosing with whom to stand at recess. There is nowhere to hide. But in the midst of all this contradiction there can be faith.

If the Word of God is first and last the word of life, then faith means to entrust myself to this Word. Despite my contradiction within myself, despite all the reasons I can find for enmity with you, despite all the reasons I can find to condemn myself, the neighbor, the stranger, despite the power of death which reaches all the way to the Table, the Font, the pulpit, and even into the Book itself — in contradiction to all this contradiction, I trust myself to the Word of life. In *On Christian Doctrine* this carries the sense of a listening and openness to God through the scriptures, even if they offend me by their demand for transformation. Despite my resistance to transformation from trusting in death, the fear of God and faith both mean to choose life and to begin the work of interpretation there.

In some ways it is difficult to say what it means to choose
life and begin there. That may be because it is so hard to imagine passionate and intentional choice of something so resistant to
explanation. Or it may be because the depth of my own compromise with death is hidden from me. The difficulty can also come
because I do not *want* to know the depth of compromise. Ultimately the difficulty may be that I do not know *how* to choose
life anymore.

To choose life and begin the work of interpretation there means
seeking to see and recognize the power of death at work for what
it is, not asking about death in an abstract and theoretical way
but immediately and practically. Let the place where you live be
the place where you ask. Who is afraid and why? Of whom are
they afraid, and of whom are *they* afraid? What does this fear lead
you to do? Who is dying because of it, and how are the sources
of their death hidden from our normal view? Who benefits from
the mystification of the deaths that surround you? Is it also you,
yourself?

To ask such questions is to risk much, maybe too much. Not
that you open yourself to the power of death (for that already
has you in its power), but that you may become aware — perhaps
more aware than ever before — of how profound a transformation begins in your very perception of the place you live every day
when you seek — even for a single hour — to choose life.

If we understand that faith is "simply" trusting ourselves to
the God of life and freedom in the face of the power of death
(even and especially in its seemingly ordinary and banal forms),
then faith finds its first realization in recognizing the truth. Indeed, without faith how could one bear to recognize the truth
at all? This is central to the understanding that faith itself, is a
gift. It is the gift by which I can bear to see and acknowledge
the truth and not recoil immediately to the false protection of the
power of death. It is by this gift that another possibility becomes

visible — even if not yet doable — a possibility by which fear is contradicted.

There should be no surprise that this possibility that contradicts death and fear is love. To live in contradiction of death and fear is to trust yourself no longer to their power, but to trust yourself instead to the power of God and love. Faith is "simply" this, and ultimately this. And this is why faith, if it is indeed *faith,* is a kind of knowledge — not of doctrine, but of the truth of the gospel — which is acquired by walking in love, in contradiction of contradiction. And this is why, as well, interpretation turns to the scripture — not in disinterestedness but with the question of how to live the faith of love.

Third step: Knowledge
Fourth step: Fortitude

On the desk sits the open Bible. The bookshelves behind you are full of commentaries, dictionaries, histories, and theologies. Each in its own way offers to help you read. Each in its own way offers knowledge and a way of knowing. But why is it *you* are reading? What do you want to know, and how do you want to know it?

The same question could be asked of and about the people who will gather on Sunday. As those shelves of books offer to help you — perhaps even in ways you don't want — you will offer to help those who have gathered. What do you want *them* to know, and how do you want them to know it?

Augustine writes so forcefully of the reader finding "nothing else in [scripture]" except the love of God and the love of neighbor as ourselves for God's sake. Nothing else? Ultimately, no. Oh, there is much more to be known, but it is finally a lesser knowledge, a lesser revelation. But the lesser knowledge obscures the greater; the lesser revelation masks the greater. However true and praiseworthy they may be, they are insufficient. Even truth becomes a lie when it stops the gaze and takes the place of God.

Even truth about God becomes a lie — perhaps the most dangerous kind, because it is true — when it is substituted for the God
toward whom it points.

> Whoever thinks that [he or she] understands the divine scrip-
> tures or any part thereof so that it does not build the double
> love of God and our neighbor does not understand it at
> all.... Whoever finds a lesson [there] that is useful to the
> building of charity, even though [one] has not said what the
> author may be shown to have intended in that place, has not
> been deceived, nor is lying in any way.
>   — *On Christian Doctrine* I.36.40

What one discovers in the scripture, however, is not only this
radical claim. You find also, as in a kind of mirror, a negative
reflection of yourself. Who has been adequate to this degree of
love? Who has bound together so inseparably the love of God,
neighbor, and self?

It is a fearsome thing to be invited from lesser love to greater,
to be summoned to a love by which in the most ordinary encounter so much is at stake. In this vision it is no exaggeration
to speak of "everything" being at stake, for that is literally what
Augustine claims. The source and goal of everything is God, he
insists. Therefore the fulfillment of everything is to be referred to
the place where together they, it, we, converge.

It is not necessary, I believe, to share Augustine's metaphysical
vision of unity in order to share the commitment to the love of
God and neighbor. Because this double love of God and neighbor
is bound together so firmly, in fact, it serves to emphasize the
irreducible and irreplaceable particularity of the neighbor. 1 John
could hardly be clearer. "Those who say, 'I love God' and hate
their brothers or sisters are liars; for those who do not love a
brother of sister whom they have seen, cannot love God whom
they have not seen. The commandment we have from [God] is
this: those who love God must love their brothers and sisters

also" (1 John 4:21–22). The otherness of God is presented in the actual person of the neighbor who is actually at hand. It is presented so directly, in fact, that this very relationship is the measure and judge of our speech. *This* is what determines the truth of our speech about God; this is where God-language is "verified." And notice this, as well: the truth is not founded upon some general notion of the limits of human knowledge, but upon God's call and command.

Whether or not our speech is lying or deceiving (such words!) is determined by our love of the actual neighbor, whose otherness is the embodiment of the otherness of God, whose person is the embodiment of the call and command to love. The force of Augustine's claim, then, is to echo the insistence of Jesus (and the interpretive tradition in which *he* already stood) that it is upon the question of love of God and neighbor that the understanding of the law and the prophets depends. It is, properly speaking, a *hermeneutical* issue. It is, properly speaking, the crucial place where spiritual practice and interpretive practice must join.

Seen in this light, the work of interpretation implicates the person of the interpreter as deeply as can be. Whatever discipline, whatever path, whatever tools, whatever walk — and whatever terms one uses to name it — must bear the question of love. In the face of such a question, Augustine acknowledged, the interpreter recognizes his or her own fragility and incompleteness, and the language through which this comes to expression is lament. The weakness of my love (no matter how great its strength), the partiality and incompleteness of my love (and how could it be otherwise, since I am partial and incomplete?), the scatteredness and division of my love (which divides the world into what is loved and what is not) confront the reader of the scripture and bring the reader to the judgment of fear.

Let us recognize that there is a fear that is loyal to life, and for the sake of life. There is a fear that resounds in us as the alarm of life itself calling out in the face of what would destroy life. While one might usually think of this as a fear in response to the threat from outside, it can also be in response to the threat from within. As in the case of this fear Augustine names in the face of my own lack of love, the alarm comes from the recognition of how it stands between me and my neighbor (and therefore between me and God).

Fear itself *is* the judgment. It is the mark of recognition, the implicit confession of the lack of love. So strong is the power of this fear — because it is a judgment pronounced within ourselves where it cannot be evaded — that consolation cannot be found within oneself, and in fear (for how else could the fearful person come?) one calls out to God for strength against the triumph of fear, which is called despair.

Now, however, comes a strange turn. One asks for consolation against despair, Augustine says, and what you are given to fortify you is a hunger and thirst for justice. The mourning is comforted by hunger; strange comfort. In the face of love one laments the lack of love. In mourning one turns for comfort and strength. For comfort and strength one is given a hunger and thirst for justice.

This hunger and thirst for justice turns your eye from the fascinating captivity to what is ephemeral. For what else is it that blinds us to justice and injustice alike, but a self-deception? Whatever else injustice is, it is founded upon a self-deceiving hunger which chooses what is not love.

Here is the strange comfort of the hunger and thirst for justice: in my mourning of the weakness of my love, I can ask for a comfort which leaves me consoled *to* my lack of love, at peace with my lack of love. What God gives (if Augustine is believed) is a consolation that consoles by restlessness, the consolation of perpetual hunger, a consolation of no consolation. For love is not the answer. It is the question that puts an end to all answers.

I kept the snapshot that shows Bill kneeling down on the asphalt playground: short gray hair, lanyard and whistle, khaki pants, high-top sneakers. He is surrounded by children. Mimi must have taken the picture from the office window, one story above. Bill appears to be holding one of the children, whose back is turned to the camera. The faces of the others register something like concern.

"Friendly House" was what the building was called. It was four stories of old brick, with a gym, playrooms for kids, classrooms with sewing machines, typewriters, art materials, a kitchen for cooking, offices for private appointments. A couple of blocks upwind stood the packing plant, from which drifted down the sounds and smells of the slaughterhouse. The top floor was Bill and Mimi's apartment. Friendly House was where they lived.

"Social workers" was what Bill and Mimi were called by higher-ups or agency folks, perhaps because they weren't sure what else to put on the job descriptions or grant proposals. Ask the children and they'd tell you Bill and Mimi were the Friendly People.

I met them through a summer job in college. I was a young man who could come and go each day and walk away at the end of August, then return the following June, a year closer to the next Big Choice in life. The children, however, couldn't just walk away, and Bill and Mimi didn't. The children were there because they were poor. Bill and Mimi were poor because they were there.

One night they invited me for supper upstairs. We made small talk for a while, and drank iced tea. Finally, they asked me what I planned to do after college. Maybe ministry, I told them, although I wasn't very clear about what that really meant, and what was required. I remember Bill and Mimi exchanging glances, and Mimi nodding her head, as if to give Bill some kind of permission.

"Mimi and I are Christians, too," he said.

"Is that why you're here?"

"That's right," Mimi answered. "Jesus loved the little children." She looked back at Bill.

"What kind of ministry do you want to do?" he asked.

I didn't know what to say, and I don't recall how I answered. Probably something vague about helping people, but nothing that was a thousandth part as real as a day in Bill and Mimi's life. That's why I kept the photograph: a snapshot of the question of love.

Fifth step: The counsel of mercy
Sixth step: Love of the enemy
Seventh step: Wisdom

The hunger and thirst for justice, as Augustine envisions it, is drawn forward by a distant glow, which is at once too bright to look upon and obscured by the stain of the reader's own eyes. Augustine does not doubt that there is truth, but the truth that draws him forward keeps escaping his sight because the eye of his mind is clouded by an appetite for something less than truth. To reach for a term from this time, self-interest contaminates, distracts, protests, even recoils from the truth. The reader's self-interest struggles against the consolation of the justice hunger and prefers a consolation within itself. If the interpreter is to go forward it must be by a fifth step: the counsel of mercy.

In some ways we may imagine mercy as something we ourselves enact, and that is true. One person extends mercy to another and loves another. Yet in a different sense, it is mercy that acts upon us. Love transforms the lover. Love is not *mine* that I should give it or withhold it. What do you hold when you withhold love? What do you keep? You keep an absence; you hold *nothing*. *Nothing* can have a shape, a weight; you can hold *nothing* in your hand. There is an immediacy to *nothing*. The mathematicians have it right: zero is a real number, as real as one. You can choose *nothing*, possess *nothing*, and even be *nothing*. That is the burden of Paul's words when he repeats in so many ways that without love he gains, possesses, and becomes *nothing*. It is not that he *isn't* anymore; he is. But he is *nothing*.

The counsel of mercy is the transformation worked in you by the love of the neighbor, and just so the distorting power of solitary self-interest can find no secret entry Augustine insists that the transforming power which love works upon the lover intends to strengthen you into love of the enemy.

Now the *power* of fear is most plainly confronted. The enemy is the particular and immediate embodiment of my fear. In one sense, it is not my enemy who makes me afraid; it is my fear which makes the other my enemy. What makes the other my *enemy* is that in this other I must face my fear itself, the very force that seeks to separate me from God, the other, and myself.

As enemy, the other is Godless, because as I meet the other as enemy I meet my own Godlessness. The love of the enemy, therefore, is the clearest site of the struggle for transformation. Indeed, how it stands between me and my enemy is how it stands between me and the "world." To die to the world in this sense, is to die to the world of enmity, to die to the world defined by fear. "To die" signals how complete the claim of fear is upon life, how profound the struggle against the power of fear is, and how radical such transformation is.

Seen in this light, the work of interpretation *is* the conflict with the power of Godlessness and death. And if we follow Augustine, that conflict is first of all within the interpreter. Rather than being temporarily set aside in favor of a more "objective" enquiry, such conflict is directly engaged at the outset and is contested at every point. The spiritual discipline of interpretation *requires* it. Augustine insists that the true objectivity — that is, seeing things as they are to the extent they can be seen — happens only by a "cleansing of the eye of the heart" through the discipline of loving the neighbor and the enemy. Through this alone can one come to see (and only to the extent one's heart is cleansed) neighbor, enemy, self, and truth as they are.

What do we call this place of arrival of this discipline? Augustine calls it wisdom. Not vision, not revelation or knowledge, but wisdom. As wisdom it can be received, but not given; learned, but not taught. It is not a map, but the land itself.

Here Augustine's discussion comes quickly to an end. No explanation of wisdom is offered. He only says that the gift of wisdom is peace and tranquility. Instead of struggle? He doesn't say. How could that be? No, but a measure let us say, so that even in the midst of the struggle what one presses toward is already given.

This is the method Augustine places before the interpreter of scripture. Now there is more to his method and more to understand about signs, figures, ambiguity, conventions, rules of inference, combination, and discovery, but everything that unfolds as he thinks through the (already ancient) issues of interpretation stands within this claim of love. No matter how obscure, puzzling, complex, or contradictory the text may be, there is finally a *sayable* meaning, a meaning that can be depended upon, to the words of the text. There is an ultimate meaning to which true interpretation leads, and that meaning is intelligible, even if the text and intermediary meanings are not. The destination of all scriptural words is love. What kind of *method* is this? One that is at once difficult, radical, and simple.

The method is difficult because love is what is most difficult. If love is the greatest commandment, then surely it is because no commandment could ask more; if love is the greatest obedience, then surely it is because no obedience requires more. If love is the greatest freedom, then surely that is because it recognizes no greater claim. This is more than the ordinary difficulty of hard tasks; there is a fundamental difficulty that comes from bringing together *command* and *love*. What kind of love can be commanded? What kind of command is it that can only be fulfilled in love? If I do what I do in obedience, then how is that love? If I do what I do in love, then what is the need for obedience? To speak of the method as difficult means to speak what cannot be resolved and *remains* difficult.

The method is radical because love is what is most radical. How do you obey the God who gives freedom if not by being free? If love is the greatest freedom, then surely it is because there is no greater freedom than to be free *for*. Freedom is not the possibility of choosing; freedom chooses. This is an old truth. Only if love chooses freely is it love. Only if freedom chooses love is it freedom. That is why the method is radical: it leads us to this word "only." Strangely enough, however, this word "only" which speaks of something singled out, standing alone, standing finally, is bound to the word "all" which gathers together, joins, unites; the awful *all* of love. So when Paul writes, "Owe no one anything, except to love one another" (Rom. 13:8), it is as much as saying, "Owe no one anything except everything." Neither *only* nor *all* are radical; the radical is where *only* and *all* meet.

The method is simple because it puts to you an implacable question: does this interpretation work the work of love? It makes a sovereign claim, and stands as a permanent question mark. All explanation, all understanding, theorizing, systematizing, codifying, imagining, tearing down, building up, law and judgment, gospel and grace stand or fall on the question of love.

Augustine proposes a method which cannot become a method, because love is precisely what cannot be methodical. Love is perfectly free, perfectly bound (see Luther, "A Treatise on Christian Freedom").

From method to way, way to walk, walk to practice, practice to praxis, praxis to discipline, discipline to freedom. From fear of God to faith, faith to knowledge, knowledge through hunger for justice to fortitude in the struggle, fortitude to mercy, mercy to love of the enemy, love of the enemy to wisdom. One could think of these respectively as formal and material *descriptions of a transformative spirituality of interpretation.* Or one could think of them as transformations by which the salvation of a preacher is worked out in fear and trembling. Or one could think of them as the terms and conditions of what is at stake in the seemingly simple and ordinary task of reading the scripture and preparing to speak. If Augustine's description (or my interpretation) of what is necessary as spiritual work seems wrong to you, let it go for now. If it does nothing more at this moment than raise the intensity of the question, that is enough.

The intensity of the question is raised most directly by putting it to yourself. This particular day in which the work of interpretation begins again, how will you undertake it?

Two

A Life of Interpretation

The life of interpretation ◆ The middle ◆ Inwardness ◆ Relationship ◆ Thou ◆ Situation ◆ Embodiment ◆ Totality, Infinity, and the Face ◆ Self-understanding

Another morning. Walk down to the café and see who might be there. Walk past the houses of people you know, and others you have seen but never met. It doesn't take much of a guess to know that in each house there is suffering; some of it you know — perhaps even better than the people who live there — some you can surmise from the usual signs. In one house the pain is in the body. In another it is between two people. In another it is a suffering mind or spirit. The causes may be as immediate as a stumble on the stairs or as distant as foreign war, as personal as friendship or as impersonal as a trade treaty. What has been happening in these houses while you sat before the open Book? Has your ear been opened to listen to what you will hear?

At the café it is the regulars plus a few strangers. A group of retired men sit in the smoking corner and thump the floor with canes to make their points. Two women rest their elbows on a small table, cradle their cups in front of their faces and lean their heads close to speak. A young man in paint-splattered coveralls sits alone at the counter and stares absently at the backlit photo of a mountain stream hung just above the soda dispenser. What have

41

these people been doing while you read and wondered? What questions would they put to you?

In the afternoon it is the hospital: one birth, one broken hip, one biopsy awaiting results. Each room is thick with memory and possibility, all of it scary in a different way. One family asks to pray. One speaks about sports. One seems embarrassed by your presence. The chapel is empty; the waiting rooms are full. The television is on.

Late in the afternoon it is back to the study, to the Book again. Your attention keeps wandering to the houses, the faces, the conversations. Through the window can be seen the top floor of the building across the street. Framed by sky and clouds, the brick glows in the low sun, and the windows flash white. It is rather beautiful, in fact, if a person takes time to look. As dusk comes only the reading light upon your desk remains on, making a small circle of light for the Book, the pad of yellow paper, the pencil, your hands.

In the evening it is the Council. Topics include estimates for the boiler, the youth group's latest offense to sensibilities, a proposal for joining the network of homeless shelters this winter, and the first draft of next year's budget, including the question of what to do about your salary. There is much discussion of the boiler, much concern about the shelter, much head-shaking about the youth, much discomfort about the budget. The people around the table are honest about their dislikes and apprehensions. They are doing what seems to them right to do. They also seem disappointed in themselves, as if they wished they knew how to do better, or had the courage to do what they already knew. That is a disappointment with which you are not unfamiliar in yourself. Who isn't? From where does such courage come? What does it have to do with the yellow pad on your desk and the days between now and Sunday?

At the end of the evening you return home to the faces, voices, and aromas of your own house, the pictures on your walls, the novel on the table. In bed with the light out, the matters of the day begin to come loose from their particularity and blend into one another. The words fade together, the characters change places, the times become anytime, and everywhere becomes here. Nine lepers leave the hospital without looking back. Twelve-year-old Jesus astounds the old men at the café. John the Baptist steps into an icy mountain stream. Where the day leaves off and the dreams begin again is impossible to tell. It has been an ordinary sort of day.

The life of interpretation

The life of ministry is a life of interpretation. Reading the face on the street, in the kitchen, in the mirror. Listening for the meaning of a sigh, or the falling tone in a person's voice. Leaning over the fence at the schoolyard to watch the swirl of young lives already dancing out figures of the future. Pondering the picture on the front page, turning off the TV to gather images together. Reading the Bible, preparing to preach.

Each dimension of experience, to be sure, poses special challenges and requires different methods, different disciplines, different help. The interpretation of the singular life, the life shaped in its particular archeology of desire and pain and hope, living in its particular storied world, speaking in its particular dialect of the heart, this life makes one kind of requirement. The interpretation of the life of human communities emerging through certain histories, responding to certain pressures and possibilities and limits, meeting and conflicting and shaping new futures, this makes a different kind of requirement. The interpretation of the greater meaning, purpose, and goal of our own lives and life itself — the dimension of ultimacy, or depth, or spirit, or mystery — this makes a different requirement still.

Each of these dimensions of human experience brings forward its different "texts," each requires its particular ways of

understanding, each makes different demands upon one's thinking, feeling, loving, caring, courage, it is true. But they are finally
only different moments of the same work of interpretation. Although the face, the children, the statistics, and the scripture
make different demands, in the end for the preacher their interpretation must be framed in words, and those must be words
spoken. For the preacher all the "multitudinous" interpretation
must come to the same moment: the moment of speaking. It
is this speaking moment that makes all the interpretation real.
There in the middle of life one person testifies to another. Having read what has been read, having seen what has been seen,
having felt what has been felt, having thought what has been
thought, from the middle of what *could* be nothing more than
chaos or nonsense, one person risks speaking a word, as little or
as much as that might be. Interpretation becomes real through
speaking.

And how does speaking become real? "For the sake of a
single poem," Rilke wrote, "you must..." and he began a
marvelous and terrifying catalogue of experience: cities, people,
losses, deaths, love. So much to experience, at the end of which
one "might perhaps be able to write ten good lines."[1] The catalogue sounds so daunting and the requirement a single poem
makes so heavy, it is easy forget that what he describes as so
extraordinary is in reality less than what the work of ministry
leads you into whether you want it to or not. In some ways
Rilke's depiction falls short, in fact, because in ministry we are
rarely permitted simply to experience, but are called upon in the
midst of experience to interpret. If speaking is to become real it
does so because of its power to interpret the actual terms of our
lives.

Interpretation for preaching is clearly more than the decipher-
ing of biblical texts and what they may have meant; this is
certainly no new insight. So often, however, preaching is content with the most general application set amid thin and barely

real anecdotes. The interpretation is of the text of the Bible, but not of the text of actual life, the actual terms of existence of the community in all its ordinariness, splendor, pain, and particularity. I take it for granted that to read and grasp what is at stake in a book — any book, not just the Bible — will require me hours and days, often for only the most tentative grasp. Even after so much time I will have to return again and again to engage the text from a different angle, with a different question. Yet I may suppose that I can read and understand the "text" of the playground, of the face, of the street corner with no such discipline and struggle, with no such commitment and focused attention.

Preaching becomes just as empty when it misunderstands the people as when it misunderstands the scriptures. Preaching loses its way just as much when it fails to take seriously the ordinary claims of experience as when it disregards the claims of the scriptures. If I have not interpreted the Bible for and with the time and place at hand, I have offered only the dead letter. The irony is that the preaching that has misunderstood the people *must* misunderstand the Bible. This is more than a general appeal for relevance; it is a demand placed upon the preacher by the Christian proclamation itself in its concreteness and embodiment.

"Preaching should have of all things the very closest relationship to existing," wrote Kierkegaard.[2] His concern was that preaching had become "poetic." It falsified actual life by presenting it shorn of its ordinariness, boredom, ambiguity, confusion, and suffering. Even worse, he believed, preaching took the reality of Jesus and betrayed it in the same way. The suffering of Jesus is covered over in the pastels of a happy ending. The actuality of rejection, abandonment, and death — not as the preparation for revelation, but as the means of it — is eclipsed by glory. In doing so, preaching strips away the very scandal and offense by which God communicates and summons humankind to faith. Everything that makes faith distinctly what it is flows from the *actuality* of existence — whether that of Jesus or of those who follow Jesus. "All essential knowledge relates to existence, or only such knowledge as has an essential relationship to existence is essential knowledge."[3]

This does not mean, however, that existing is the same as being given over to the mundane, whether comfortable or painful. The day to day can be as much an evasion of existence as the poetic. It is precisely in the tension between the seemingly impossible news of the gospel and ordinary life that Christian existence moves. Even the most astonishing claims and promises of the gospel must be held in relationship to ordinary life, and it is there in the contradiction that both ordinary life and the gospel are what they are. Indeed, it is in such contradiction and paradox that *existing* occurs, Kierkegaard insisted. To the extent that life is content with either the mundane or the poetic, to that extent it falls away from existence. "Existence is the child that is born of the infinite and the finite, the eternal and the temporal, and is therefore a constant striving" (*Postscript,* p. 85).

To claim that preaching should have of all things the very closest relationship to existing, therefore, is to make a profound demand. It demands that preaching speak from and toward the actual life that is summoned beyond itself and to itself by the scandal of the gospel. Preaching must speak of ultimate things in immediate terms. The café, the meeting, the hospital: ordinary life regarded as the place where ultimacy is to be met, the place where the scandal of the gospel is to be understood or not at all. Whatever else preaching must do, it must speak to, of, and within the life we share. Unless I interpret the sigh, I cannot interpret the scripture. Until I read the figure unfolding on the playground, the page of the Bible will remain closed to me, no matter how open the covers appear. Unless I commit myself to telling the story of my time and place, I will have no Story of God to tell, only stories of gods.

The middle

The starting point of interpretation is always in the middle. Whether one reflects about the nature of the Bible itself or about particular texts, about the gospel and its proclamation as a whole or about one preacher, about the mission of the church or the mission of the people around the table, it is in the middle that such thinking begins. If one reflects at even a more rooted level — about what it is to be addressed, to hear, to have a Book, to read, to have a voice, to speak to another — it is in the middle that such thinking begins.

We begin in the middle of a discussion, of a story, of a sentence, a meal, a night; in the middle of a day, a sickness, a family, a house, a community, a history, a language. One begins thinking always inside a certain skin, among certain people, as a particular body. There is a world already shaped inside us and around us, a world we have helped shape and which has helped shape us. There is a world which we know only in part, and which we *know* we only know in part. That world may well be only *knowable* in part, and at both its core and rim one may sense a dimension of persistent mystery which will neither go away nor step out into the open. We begin with a *given-ness,* that is to say.

The given-ness of the already unfolding life has the feel of "if only" to it. Whether by providence or chance or some other unnamed force, the days and acts of a life have led here to this day and this beginning. They need not have. If I hadn't crossed the street, if I hadn't turned to look, if I had taken a different train, who knows? And in how many other ways might the fragility of this particular life been overwhelmed, for good and ill both? By the unknowing acts of strangers, or the intricate and intimate web of relationship? By the convulsion of violence, or by the impersonal path of the wind? There is a fantastic quality to the contingency of a real life, in which so much might be different. There is a marvelous quality to the impossibly delicate connections that make a particular life.

At the same time, there is in this given-ness a kind of necessity, too. Days did lead on to days, paths to other paths, detours became new roads. There are a million reasons that this should not, could not, ought not, have been; nevertheless, it is. This particular life is the one that has come to pass and made a story. Of all the ways it might have been, it is this particular life which has become real and tangible, and in the middle of which thinking, interpreting, preaching, and believing begins — again.

Inwardness

Christianity is spirit, spirit is inwardness, inwardness is subjectivity, subjectivity is essentially passion.

—Kierkegaard, *Postscript,* 33

To speak of the particularity of one's life would seem easy. All you do is look around, notice what is as hand, and start there. Yet what to one person is self-evidently at hand is not self-evident at all to another. Your own life can feel often as if you were walking in on the middle of a conversation, trying to guess what had just been said, and why; trying to understand where things are leading; trying to figure a way to enter that actually makes you part of the conversation, not just an onlooker. Open the Bible and the same thing happens. The text is a moment and stretching out from it on all sides is a vast discussion in every kind of voice. Step back from the text to gather your thoughts about this question or that, and it happens again, a vast conversation of interpretation and ideas. Beyond that, even farther, extend the dimensions of world and history and mystery that you can never encompass. Yet in the middle of it all one still must try to make sense. One's life is like a text in this way, as a text is like a life.

The starting place of interpretation, let us acknowledge, is the actual life of the actual interpreter. Through its transformation into the communication known as preaching, interpretation directs itself toward the actual life of the actual hearer. There in the life of the actual hearer interpretation begins again. This does not mean that interpretation is only about the speaker and the hearer, but it is *always also* about them. This, too, is part of what it means to understand interpretation as a spiritual discipline. Christian faith, Kierkegaard insisted, ultimately intends the transformation of the person in that person's most profound dimension. His name for that dimension is inwardness. The greatest claim a truth can make upon a person is an inward claim, because it is from inwardness that one's life in the world flows. Kierkegaard interpreted from his particular time and place, and tried from there to grasp something of human life and experience that might be true for him and for others, as well. He believed he was witnessing a triumph of a so-called objectivity and exteriority that simply presumed too much for itself, whether in the realm of philosophy, church, community life, or relationships. For all its complexity and apparent success, beneath the surface he saw the question of what it means to be a person stretching down into the most profound depths. The bright glare on the water concealed (and perhaps meant to conceal) the actual terms of existence, where he believed whatever truth was possible for humankind was to be met. Without inwardness there could be no truth to life, and especially to faith. Faith was for him where the question of living truth became sharpest.

The language of inwardness is so easily distorted. It can mean isolation from the neighbor, detachment from the world, absorption within oneself. Being completely absorbed into the external world is a kind of madness, he observes, and so is being completely absorbed within oneself. The powerful dialectic of inwardness and outwardness is exactly that: a perpetual reversal of pole to pole.

This can be seen most tellingly in the paradox of love. Love comes from within, he insists, from the greatest depth of the human heart. There it is hidden and cannot be seen; no matter how deep the reach, it can never come to this hidden place. Yet this hidden depth is also the hidden source from which love issues in all its different ways. Love may not be known in itself, but it *is* knowable by its fruits.[4] These fruits are deeds done in love. That they are deeds means that they are outward. That they are done in love means that they flow from inwardness. There is no word that of itself can reveal love or the motive of love. The word that bespeaks love in one mouth bespeaks hate in another. There is no deed that of itself can reveal love. The *how* of its doing makes all the difference, and the how has to do with the heart. The heart determines everything; nevertheless, it is with fruits that love must be concerned, and it is by fruits that love permits itself to be known.[5] Love shall be known by its fruits.

The direction of the spirit is inward; the direction of the truth is inward. It is inward because that is where essential transformation is rooted and only the truth and knowledge that relate to existence are essential. But relationship to the truth, as with love, cannot be known decisively in the externals, only in the heart's interior. To be changed in relationship to the truth means to be changed inwardly. The path of personhood is a path of transformation through an intensification of inwardness.

Such inward truth or essential knowledge is not something one person can really share with another. It cannot be known in the way one knows multiplication tables or the capitals of the states. One person cannot follow the path of another's inwardness. If I try to follow another's path it is no longer my own inwardness I pursue. The path of inwardness "closes behind" one, to use Kierkegaard's vivid image (*Postscript*, 62). The ground gained can never be won for another. Indeed, the very attempt to do so obstructs the crucial work of a human life. For that matter, I may not follow even my own paths if they have become fixed and static. Movement is the constant, not fixity. Becoming is the constant, not being. Inwardness is a process, and transforms everything into a process, because that is the very nature of existence, constant striving. The path of inwardness is not the path of *a* transformation (that may be finished and accomplished), but of transformation itself.

Interpretation and preaching that flow from inwardness are confronted continually with paradox. The same infinite tension that seeks to hold together the ultimate and the ordinary is at work. The quality of inwardness can be only known by the speaking and acting that have everything to do with outwardness (bound to the terms and conditions of a day like today, and whatever is at hand). Yet outwardness can only gesture toward its inward source, and never show it plainly.

The same is true for the people at the café, the hospital, and the council meeting. The clerk at the bank, the trash truck driver, and the elderly couple sitting on the bench face the same impossible pull of the infinite and the ordinary, of the truth that only each of them can know within themselves and the small repertoire of words and deeds by which they live a day. Whatever the good news may be, and whatever it means to make of us, now is the acceptable time. The day of the Lord is at hand.

Relationship

In the beginning is the relation.
— Martin Buber

Interpretation that begins in the middle of actual life is interpretation in the midst of a relational world. Who are these people who come before your mind as you prepare to preach? When you meet them, how do you meet them? When you think of them, how do you think of them? Who are you because of your relationship with them? Who are you without them?

If Kierkegaard raised the question of the individual to most intense expression, Martin Buber, whose work *I and Thou* has been so important to so many, affirmed with no less intensity the relational nature of what it is to be a person.[6] Buber wrote of two kinds of existence in relationship, each of them founded upon a primary word, or ground-word, each of them founding a different kind of world: the I-Thou and the I-It. In the beginning is the primary word of address, a primary word of encounter, presence, immediacy, a word of reception, acceptance, mutuality, of validation and value. The primary word says "Thou" and thereby makes the one who speaks an I. The primary word says "Thou" and thereby evokes the other I who responds "Thou." To call and be answered back, to hear oneself called and thereby to become oneself in responding — this establishes the world of relation (*I and Thou*, 6). Thou is an Other who is addressed whole, in the uniqueness, freedom, mystery, and unencompassable integrity of its own existence.

There is also a different world founded by a different word, the world of It. This is a world of order, distinctions, definitions, ends and means, ideas, things, goals, plans, organization, conceptions *about,* reflection *upon.* An It is viewed through lenses of knowledge and experience that inevitably reduce and distort the other to correspond to the needs and views of the I. These are by no means necessarily ignoble (although they may be). The world of It is a necessary world, without which human beings cannot live. But one who is always and only an I in the world of I-It is not fully I; without It humans cannot live; without Thou humans cannot live humanly.

These two Is are not the same. The I who addresses another as friend is different from the I who addresses another as means to an end, the bank teller who cashes your check, for instance. Indeed, the I of I-Thou is realized anew and differently according to the particular Thou who is addressed, just as I who am addressed and respond "Thou" am realized anew in new address. When I address the Thou who is my friend, it is a different I than when I address my father, and a different I than when I address my spouse.

Buber is a philosopher and theologian of realization, of making existence real in relationship with things, creation, and the particular Other.[7] It is not only other people with whom one says the word "I-Thou." It is not being a rock, a table, or a loaf of bread which makes an It (just as it is not being human which makes someone a Thou[8]); but this rock, this table, this bread can be a Thou with which I come to be myself. The same table upon which you write your words each week may belong to the world of It, and appropriately so, for what is a table for if not to use for other purposes: to hold the plate, to support the paper, a place for the lamp to sit to give you light? But sometimes you discover that you are not sitting at a table, even at *the* table, but at Table, and *this* Table is intimately and powerfully part of who you are; you discover that it is the where and when of who you are. This is a spirituality that flows along the lines of the mystery of relationship, unabashedly affirming that the human can be only human through this mystery, and that this mystery is always at hand in the presence of the other person, the world of creation, and even the ordinary objects in the midst of which we live.

The language through which Buber expresses himself (and that through which anyone might try to bring the I-Thou meeting to expression) is awkward and strange. How can you talk about something that by definition can't be talked about? Thou cannot be spoken *about*, only spoken *with*. As soon as you begin speaking *about* Thou you have begun to move into the world of I-It. As soon as I turn to speaking *about* Thou the Thou is transformed, circumscribed, an object among objects (however respected), an experience, a story, at the disposal of my speaking. This is, Buber acknowledges, the "melancholy fate" of every Thou in our world: to become an It (*I and Thou*, 16). To live continually in the world of Thou is not possible. "Every response binds up the

Thou in the world of It.... But that which has been so changed into It, hardened into a thing among things, has had the nature and disposition put into it to change back again and again" (*I and Thou*, 40). And this is another paradox, another reversal.

The transition from Thou to It may be melancholy because of the loss of immediacy and presence, but it is nevertheless a transition to a world of grave importance and vital possibility. The world of It is a world fundamental to existence, not simply a compromise with something better. The analytical methods we use to understand one another are "indispensable whenever [they] further knowledge of a phenomenon without impairing the essentially difficult knowledge of its uniqueness that transcends the valid circle of method."[9] What method cannot encompass is uniqueness; that is not the purpose of method. Knowledge of the uniqueness of the Other is *essentially difficult* and remains that way. Our analysis cannot take the place of relationship.

The world of I-Thou exceeds the I-It in the same way as love exceeds law without setting it aside. In the world of I-Thou relation the response to the Other is uniquely and distinctly particular to *this* Thou in the actual meeting at hand.

The waitress brings a piece of pie and puts it down on the counter. "Scoop of ice cream with that? No? Anything else?"

She wipes her hands with the little towel hooked on her apron. "I'm Denise," she says, pointing to a name badge. "You're the Reverend who talked at May's funeral, aren't you? I was there."

"Was she a friend of yours?"

"In a way." Denise tilts her head and narrows her eyes a little. "You said nice things about May and how she was with people. What you said was right. I know." She hesitates, then says, "You knew her. What do you think? Is someone just born that way? Or can a person change and become somebody new?"

"Well, I don't know about being born that way. I don't think May was. I think there was a lot of hard work and struggle and prayer and surprise. She was pretty amazing, but the person who was most amazed was May herself."

"Amazed at what?" Denise asks.

"At her own life. Who she used to be. Who she became."

"Who did she used to be?"

"She'd probably say that doesn't matter. She'd probably say the gospel changed her, and that's what matters."

Denise wipes her hands, looking down at them. "I want to be like her. Someday."

"So do I."

Looking out the window toward the street now, wiping her hands still, but absently she repeats, "I really do want to be like her. I really do."

Thou

The extended lines of relation meet in the eternal Thou.

— Martin Buber

Most ministers have stories to tell about how they got it all wrong and how that changed them. Sometimes the story is comic. Everything works out in the end, and you can tell it with a rueful laugh and a shake of your head: "I can't believe I did anything so dumb. Thank heavens I forgot to mail that letter!" Sometimes the story is a matter of wonder, a *there but for the grace of God go I* kind of tale in which something you did was miraculously transformed from awful into wonderful. Sometimes the story is genuinely tragic, and all you can do is to tell it as a kind of confession, repentance, and promise — to yourself if to no one else. My own such stories all seem to have a quality of missing something hidden in plain sight.

Buber once wrote of an experience he called a conversion. He had understood religious experience as the extraordinary, timeless, and ecstatic which stood outside the flow of everyday life. One morning after just such experience he received a young man who had come to talk to him. Unaware that the young man was in despair Buber talked with him attentively and openly, but without discerning what was happening with his conversation partner. Only later, after the young man's death did Buber learn that he had been sought out by someone struggling to make a profound decision. What had he needed? "Surely," Buber wrote, "a presence by means of which we are told that nevertheless there is meaning." From that time Buber gave up the so-called religious. "I possess nothing but the everyday out of which I am never taken....I know no fullness but each mortal hour's fullness of claim and responsibility."[10]

Meeting is about presence. Presence is how meaning happens. And meaning is the great "nevertheless" by which life receives the power to go forward (*I and Thou*, 110). The power of presence is meaning itself: beyond explanation, definition, solution (all of which belong to the world of It). Because it is an event of meaning, "Nothing can any longer be meaningless" (*I and Thou*, 110). This ordinary hour is where meaning happens, in relation with this world, and only this world. Yet because it is this very world (and not a world of dreams), the meaning of the world itself is assured. Meaning is within the world, not beyond it. Because there is a real presence, there is, therefore, a real present time (not simply the realms of memory and hope) and because there is a real present, eternity is *realized*. The eternal Thou is present in the I-Thou.

None of this, however, is a theory, a message, a program. It reveals no law or doctrine or solution. "We cannot approach others with what we have received and say 'You must know this, you must do this.' We can only go, and confirm its truth. And this, too, is no 'ought,' but we can, we *must*" (*I and Thou*, 111). This is Buber's understanding of revelation. And the force of this revelation is the weight of life heavy with meaning in a world where you are addressed, where you may meet in the ordinary circumstance of the day the Thou through whom you glimpse the eternal Thou in which all relations are consummated, the Thou who cannot become It (*I and Thou*, 75). The experience of I and Thou is the experience of meeting, presence, meaning, power, revelation, eternity — in the daily world.

The task of daily life, therefore, becomes the work of discernment. Buber's writings often depict this work in the most poignant ways. If the I-Thou meeting is not something that is finally describable, the failure or refusal to meet the Other certainly can be told. A despairing young man comes with a Question, yet because Buber could hear only the questions he gave only answers. They talked but they did not meet, and in the end the young man was left alone with his despair. A worker at a public gathering makes a statement with implications that Buber refutes, yet in his eagerness to refute the statement he silences the questioner. In many such stories Buber presents the difficulty and importance of discernment, in many such stories that you who do this work yourself can tell, as can I.

"If we had a keen vision and feeling of all ordinary human life, it would be like hearing the grass grow and the squirrel's heart beat, and we should die of that roar that lives on the other side of silence," observes the narrator in George Eliot's *Middlemarch*.[11] What a remarkable image of what lies on the other side of silence, the other side of ordinary life! Little wonder that one might pull back from such an overwhelming roar. Little wonder we miss it, and perhaps even *try* to miss it. The world on *this* side of silence is necessary, after all, and there are things to be done. The bank teller wants to cash your check, not tell you his life story with six people behind you in line. And you want the check cashed, too. This is not the time to look questioningly into the other person's eyes and sincerely ask how things are. Indeed, nothing may or should happen beyond the ordinary transaction, yet the truth remains. Something eternal is at hand, because this other person is near. And sometimes without knowing how or why, despite one's own best and worst efforts, we find that in the midst of everything the grace of meeting happens. Meeting, presence, meaning, power, revelation, eternity: all this weight of possibility bearing upon the events and encounters of an ordinary day. And since this ordinary day includes preparing to preach, the weight of possibility is there, too.

Situation

Discernment, then, is necessary, but discernment of what? The French philosopher Gabriel Marcel proposes that the I-Thou meeting takes place in a *situation*.[12] The realization of I-Thou, is in relation not only to each other, but to each other in a shared circumstance. To meet, to enter in mutuality and response, means to grasp what is at stake (at the *heart* is Marcel's phrase) in who, when, where, with, and among whom we are. This does not mean to share an analysis, plan, or action (which indeed may grow from meeting). It is meeting and presence that gathers its weight, its meaningfulness, precisely because of the situation, the history in which we meet.

The present is not some eternal "Everymoment," timeless, occurring whenever and wherever. The present is not *any* present but *this* one. There are those in whom I have met Thou, and the meeting was in the midst of very difficult struggle. The presence and power of relationship was confirmed in the terms of conflict in which we had to act, without being defined, limited, or exhausted by the particularity of the struggle. Yet at the same time, without the struggle — like the young person's despair in which he sought out Buber — *this* meeting in the present could not happen. In the same way the struggle itself is both altered and realized as the situation in which this meeting has occurred.

As Buber saw in the years after *I and Thou,* the question put to one through the speech of the situation is God's question, a question through which the Eternal Thou speaks. We should recognize, therefore, that not only people, creation, art, things, but also events are capable of becoming the partner of the Word which grounds existence as I-Thou. There are times in which we come to ourselves and to one another, knowing who we are and what we must do. Perhaps that is why a person or a whole generation or even a nation can dwell in the past. That past is so much a part of their identity and relationships that to let go of it means (one fears) to lose one's very self. Yet to hold on means to deny my responsibility in the present, to those present. What meaning could responsibility have that does not include a responsibility to the hour and the story in which we meet and are met? Interpretation takes place in the middle of a time when those around you are trying to understand the reason for their own lives now. What is it time for us to do? How we answer the demand of the time will show us who we are, and what it means for us to be in relationship.

The phone again. One more may be one too many, especially if it's like the last one. Deep breath. In this world you will have trouble....

"Hello."

"Hey, pastor, I thought you might need a little help."

"Oh, Paul, it's you." Exhale. "Yeah, it's been a hard couple days."

"Well, I heard that maybe things got kind of rough on the shelter business. You don't have to carry this one alone, you know."

"What do you mean?"

"Other people care about it, too. And actually, some of us may be better at handling parts of this than you are. No offense."

"No, no. None taken."

"The question is whether you're willing to let something go so that can happen. Or do you just like to keep banging your head on the wall? I've heard that some ministers do. No offense."

"No offense. My head's pretty sore right now."

"So that's 'yes' to a little help?"

"I don't know what to say. Yes. Thank you. Yes."

"Thursday night? Seven? Our house?"

"Of course, yes. Certainly. Yes. Seven. I'll be there. Thank you . . . Paul, why are you doing this?"

"No big mystery. It's the right thing to do. We'll see you then."

But it is a mystery. A great mystery.

Embodiment

When we meet and are met, we do so as embodied creatures. Whatever else it may mean to be a person and to be in relationship, it has everything to do with our bodies.

Relational life, Gabriel Marcel urges, is incarnate, embodied life.[13] Self, body, and world are all connected, for good and ill both. They are not finally the same, nor are they finally separate. To speak of myself is to speak as a particular incarnation, in a place and time among others in the world of what can come in contact with my body. Embodiment is how a person participates in the world, acts and is acted upon, feels, connects, distinguishes. The experience of the body, Marcel contends, is prior to the relationship of communion, the I-Thou. The experience of the body situates us in a shared reality, a We-reality, an experience of greater community and world that allows the I-Thou to emerge.[14] The communion of I-Thou occurs through embodiment. Even when we move to the level of transcendence, when one ponders questions of ultimacy, this too, depends upon embodiment.[15] A striking insistence, with radical implications. Our bodies are the foundation of relationship, and the means of relationship, including relationship with God.

At the council meeting what was it that was so troubling about the shelter proposal? It wasn't the cost or inconvenience or principle of the thing. It wasn't the *idea* of people with no place to sleep, or the *idea* of giving food or clothes. The people around the council table were mostly generous people. It was the bodies. It was the reality that bodies would bring. Sickness, fatigue, wounds old and new. Bodies that might be dangerous or cause injury. Bodies that need to be washed. Bodies that suffer. Bodies that cannot be ignored. Bodies that have history written upon them in scars. The bodies of men, women, teenagers, children. Bodies that show the truth of how it really is among us and between us. Bodies that present the question of justice, whether divine or human. Bodies that declare, simply by their presence, that we are in relationship. Most important, bodies that would implicate us in *our* bodies.

Our bodies are means of sympathy, empathy, connection, identification, of understanding ourselves and others. Our bodies provide the capacity to feel what others feel in their bodies, a capacity for mutuality and compassion. The denial of my own body leads me to the denial of the bodies of others. If I seek to love my neighbor as myself but blank out the truths of my own physical life, how much easier it is to blank out the truths of my neighbor's physical life. Recognition of my own body, while it may not yet lead me to compassion, at least provides the possibility.

Body is both power and vulnerability, possibility and particularity. By my physical presence I act and shape the world, and through my physical presence the world also acts upon and shapes me. My body is the inescapable representation of my capacity for wounding and being wounded, caring and being cared for. Old body, young body, well body, sick, beautiful, unremarkable, smooth, scarred, female, male, darker, lighter: the dimensions of embodiment are all possibilities for reciprocity and compassion, power and vulnerability.

The capacity to feel and the awareness of vulnerability, however, do not necessarily lead to compassion and community. I see suffering, feel it, and wish to protect myself from it. I protect myself by withdrawing from those whose presence re-awakens my fear — not because I do not feel, but because I do, and I am afraid. I hope (believe is too strong and confident, fear is not so easily fooled) that I thereby save myself, and I do in a way. But the self that is saved is radically diminished, perhaps even no self at all, because it is cut off from the physical foundation of its life in the world. Incarnational, relational life is a way of "belonging to oneself precisely by belonging to the other-than-self — which identifies it" (Levinas).[16] The very physical presence of the Other is itself the embodiment of my responsibility. It is, strictly speaking, an *ethical* claim. "Ethics begins . . . as I like to put it, before the face of the other."[17] Physical presence means actual responsibility (whether I want it or not). It demands allegiance, being *for* the other.

When the work of interpretation takes place as a solitary effort, in the quiet of the study, let's say, with perhaps the *image* or *idea* of others in one's imagination, does that lure us to what is merely an *image* or *idea* of responsibility, too? And does that lead one to preach the *image* or *idea* of responsibility? And do the listeners take away a beautiful image or a well-honed idea to be turned over in their minds? Perhaps the study should be the last place one goes to prepare to preach, not the first. What would a spiritual discipline of interpretation look like that required physical presence, proximity to the neighbor and the stranger?

Totality, Infinity, and the Face

Open the church photo directory and pick any page. The faces of the people there are all known to you in a way, yet also quite unknown. How much have you really understood about any of them, and how have you taken those fragments of understanding and blown them up life-size? Sit at the café counter among the familiar and unfamiliar faces. Pick one you know and try to name the categories and quantifiers that construct that person in your imagination. What is the story in your own mind that you always recall, and by doing so, bind them to it once again? Pick a stranger and try to name the assumptions that have already begun their work in your mind. How can we understand the effects that these constructions and assumptions work upon both ourselves and the Other? How do they affect our relationship with one another and with God? Jesus taught that harm begins with a word spoken silently in one's own mind (Matt. 5:21–28), as does responsibility.

The Other is not to be essentialized and reduced, Levinas insists. The Other is not to be constrained into the cramped spaces of sameness — what we already think and think we know. That is a way of evading the Other in his or her fullness and complexity, and evading the claim that the Other's presence makes upon me. On another hand, mystery can readily become mystification. Response and responsibility then become abstractions without embodied content, a different kind of evasion. The concern not to reduce the Other to his or her need and vulnerability turns into a refusal of tangible response.

This is a genuine dilemma. A person comes to you in need, and it is imperative that you recognize and understand that person's need in order to respond. Yet the more deeply you see the need, the more it draws your attention and determines your relationship. The more it determines your relationship, the more you both are defined by it. As one who responds to needs, I need your need to be who I am. I need you to be needy. Yet the need is genuine, and deserving of response. Perhaps this is the challenge of giving in such a way that the right and left hands do not know what the other is doing. Giving as if one were not giving. Giving as if returning something that was never yours.

Levinas uses the odd pair of terms "totality" and "infinity" to name this tension. "Totality" refers to the drive toward totalization, subsuming the different and the particular under the categories and concepts of a larger whole. In such a movement the Other is reduced to certain characteristics or attributes, identified with and by them, and relegated to a scheme of relations and hierarchies, in a universe of meaning and value which is all-encompassing. Totalization has a quality of violence, figuratively and literally. It cuts off and suppresses what cannot be accounted for within its frame, and therefore violates the Other by attempting to transform it into the Same. The Same attempts to erase the Other by taking away its difference. The ultimate expression of this is murder — now we are not speaking figuratively but literally.

"Infinity," by contrast, refers to the excess and difference that refuse totalization. Infinity cannot be contained, subsumed, or fixed into hierarchies. Infinity can be neither dismissed nor fulfilled. Within a framework of totality, my responsibility toward the Other can be discharged — precisely because it corresponds to this reduction or that, and is therefore limited (a limited liability as the lawyers might say). Responsibility that responds beyond totality to the unqualifiable quality of infinity is, well, infinite too. There is no end to responsibility before the infinite. It cannot be discharged, and it cannot be ignored. The obligation to the Other has the force of a command that is embodied in the face of the Other. The human face, Levinas presses, is the place of encounter with this infinity.

The face refuses reduction, especially in resistance to my powers of totalization and murder. The other "opposes to me the infinity of his [or her] transcendence."[18] The face of the Other presents the greatest temptation in the sphere of life, the temptation of murder. It does so by virtue of both its vulnerability and its absolute resistance to possession. It is near but cannot be grasped. It is small but exceeds all limits. It is vulnerable, even destitute, yet it speaks, even without speaking, from a transcendent height. "This infinity, stronger than murder, already resists us in his [or her] face, in his [or her] face is the primordial expression, is the first word: 'thou shalt not kill.' "[19] This command is both particular and universal. It is given in the particular face of the Other, which always exceeds its particularity, so that it is both this singular face and the face of humanity. "The presence of the face, the infinity of the other is a destituteness, a presence of the third party, that is the whole of humanity which looks at us."[20] Just as the face of the other is particular and infinite, so is my responsibility. It is infinite because it concerns the infinite other. It is particular, because it is not transferable to another: it is *mine*. What I have in the encounter with the other is not the other, but my responsibility in the face of the other.[21] And in having this particular and infinite responsibility (through the encounter with the particular and infinite other), I am who I am. "Life receives meaning from an infinite responsibility, a fundamental *diacony* that constitutes the subjectivity of the subject."[22]

We know this word "diacony" from other places. In the simplest sense it means service. The challenge from Levinas is to understand this service as both making us who we are and demonstrating who we are. The vocabulary may be philosophical but the content is utterly theological and diaconal. Spiritual practice is diaconal practice, which is what responsibility means. Diaconal practice (or the lack of it) is the actual interpretation of our texts. If there is to be revelation, there is where it will be.

In the photo directory infinity is at stake. At the café counter infinity is at stake. Infinite responsibility before the human face of God. Infinite responsibility that must be acted upon concretely in the present. Time, place, relationship, body, situation, history, the Word, the face. What practice of interpretation can prepare a person for the ordinary meeting of infinity? What can prepare a person for infinite service to the Infinite?

Self-understanding

We have been considering what it means to say that interpretation begins in the middle, moving from individual life, to relational and situational life, to embodied life, and the face of the other. Call them marks from which to take bearings, recognizing that none of these different depictions of what it means to be a person may by themselves represent where we are. By plotting them out, however, and seeing how you or I stand in relation to each one of them — the distance, the angle, their relation to one another — we can know better where we stand and in what direction we are moving. The question at hand could be called the question of an interpreter's self-understanding and its implication for interpretation. Let us step back for a time and draw some of these themes together.

As an interpreter I have formed an identity in relationship to others and the world.[23] Some of this I could name explicitly, much of it I could not. I live in a world that in many ways seems simply self-evident to me. It is not open for discussion or question because it has not for me been *called* into question. My identity is formed within a culture and a tradition, so it is properly speaking a communal identity as well as personal, rooted in forces of society and history as much as my individuality. I continually enact the life of that tradition in ways that I do not see. Some of my self-understanding, however, is quite conscious. There are values, commitments, fears, perspectives, approaches that I have chosen and nurtured and cultivated. I have told myself into a particular story, told and re-told in consistent variations. Aware or unaware, however, they are always present in my self-understanding.

This self-understanding is in some ways a barrier. It creates different kinds of empty places, silent places, omissions, erasures. It overwrites the difference and particularity of otherness, and imposes my sameness upon it. The self-evident world of my understanding closes off vital possibilities without my even being aware of them and leads me into interpretations that are constantly circling back upon themselves, confirming what I already think.

In other ways, however, my self-understanding is also a bridge. It leads me to discover in the texts that surround me questions that matter, and help that is truly help. Because I am who I am, because of the terms of world and experience I inhabit, there is a place in which interpretation and understanding are possible — indeed, necessary. One's self-understanding becomes the very condition for an encounter with something that is different. The grasp of the particularity of my own life, that is, can *clear* a space (and not simply erase or overwrite) where the other can be met as an Other. By the same token, it can prevent me from erasure or overwriting as well.

By imagination or reflection I may attempt to reach backward toward some other beginning, a viewpoint more solid seeming and fundamental, a standpoint more worthy seeming, or blessed. I may try to reach back to something less embarrassing, more properly originary, which seems more serious because it is more detached from my particular fragility and odd persistence. In the same way I may imagine or think myself forward toward something more full and mature, something with the feel of completion to it, the peculiar shine and invulnerability ideas have when they are not yet embodied. I may attempt to think myself outward with no recognizable reference to myself, only speaking about texts "in themselves" as I suppose. I may think myself inward by means of a kind of reflection that I feel is purely interior, intellectual, uncompromised by the flesh I am and the world I walk in. The particular embodied and embedded life, however, for all its embarrassing concreteness and entangled ambiguity remains the real source, the necessary starting point, and the most immediate context of interpretation.

So the Bible lies open upon the table. You sit before the text alone, or at least as the only person in the room. Whatever interpretation itself is, and whatever this time of interpretation will lead to, there is clearly more than textual decipherment going on. It may be, in fact, that what is at stake is indeed *constitutive*, to use a clumsy word: world-making, self-making, community-making. How you read the text is how you read the world. How you read the text is how you read the face in the mirror, the faces on the street, the faces at the café, the faces on the evening news. How you listen, how you answer when another calls, how you bind or loose, how you take up your place and your responsibility. How you walk in the dark with the Word and the Name. If these are not your spiritual praxis, what is?

Three

The Mystery of Language

In the middle of language ◆ Speaking a world ◆ Breaking
the bonds of deadly words: The preparation of freedom ◆
Re-membering ◆ The poesis of life ◆ From the mystery of
language to the language of mystery ◆ The mystery of God ◆
Word and God ◆ God and truth ◆ To believe the Word ◆ Listening
for the Word

It is morning once again. Once again you sit at the desk with the
Book open in front of you. Some of the words are underlined;
notes are printed in small letters in the margin, many of them
several years old. On the yellow pad there are the current jottings,
an idea, an image, someone's name with "the story about the
stranger" written next to it. A line from a hymn is there, followed
by a question mark. There is a book about prayer you've been
reading, and a phrase from it over which you have wondered is
copied out onto the page, too. Anyone else but a preacher would
look at the page and figure there wasn't much there. But another
preacher would see this page of jottings differently: each mark,
each word leads back and back, and out and out, in ever widening
circles. Each one is the beginning of a journey into language with
roads and destinations as unique as the writing by which they're
inscribed. Already on the page the power and mystery of speech
is at work.

At eleven o'clock your appointment comes. It is someone you know well, whose family you know well, too: three generations. You have talked together before about what she says, because you are the only person she has been able to talk to about it. She repeats the awful things that have been said to her and how she mostly believed them. It is plain how crippled her life has been. But something else is happening, too. As she repeats you can hear that she no longer believes those things, not like she did before. She is telling it differently now, as if talking about someone who is remembered, a person from the past. The voice seems different now, stronger. Something is happening among the words inside her; something is happening that you can hear.

Walking to lunch you wait at the corner for the light to change. That hymn tune from the page is rehearsing itself, a good tune in waltz time, not much for marching but a nice lilt for dancing. A car pulls up to the stoplight, window down, music loud. The song is full of hatred and contempt. Thousands of people may be listening to it at this moment. Thousands of people will sing it and commit it to memory. What happens when we take in such songs and walk around with their words playing in our heads? Where does such a song live in one's body, and how does it lead a person to move? In the drugstore you open a popular book on the rack next to the horoscopes and crosswords. The meager and banal story written there is one through which people will understand their lives because they know of no better story to live by. This, too, is part of the mystery and power.

So is this: at the café three women sit alone together at a table in the back. One of them begins speaking, sometimes looking down, sometimes looking off into an empty corner, sometimes staring as if there were a distant horizon to be seen through the wall. The other two reach to touch her hands clasped upon the table. The first woman listens and begins to weep. It seems like something that has waited a long time to come, and it seems like something that is hard but also wonderful. Ask them what happened and they'd tell you, "Oh, we just talked about some things." That's true. It is clear that more than just talking took place, but whatever happened, just talking was *how* it happened.

In another part of town (according to the paper on the counter), in the aftermath of a tragic death full of implications, a community will gather and wait for someone to speak. As you eat lunch, in a house in the next block decisions must be made which may well hold the power of life and death. Sitting in the front room the family listens for words to be said that will help them decide how to honor the wishes of the grandmother who can no longer speak for herself. Nearby, the remnant of a congregation will gather this evening. They all are wondering how to make sense of what is happening among them and go on. Someone has been asked to tell the story once again which tells where they come from, who they are, who they are called to be.

All around you and without your knowing, the mystery and power of speech unfolds: on printed pages, in conversations, speeches, over the radio, on the TV, in hymns and songs, on billboards, and in solitary recitations which no one hears but the one who speaks.

In the middle of language

We live in the middle of language.[1] We live within language in the immediate sense of the actual words one says in a day, hears, reads. There are words we know and use to accomplish the thousand tasks of a day, ones we count upon to be understood and responded to in the usual ways. There are the words we live with as expressions of who we are, the ones by which I speak my identity to myself and to you, sometimes to my own surprise. There are the words we may not know, but which shape the world in profound ways and to which we are accountable: laws that tell what we may and may not do, declarations that make war and peace. There are the words that announce to us events and thereby make them part of one's world, and words by which we respond to events, and thereby say what they are, and *how* they are part of one's world. There are words that don't have much sense to them in the usual way, but which express and celebrate and lament, as a kind of speaking without speaking. There are words by which we try to encompass experience, and talk of history and the beginning and the end, and the reason for it all. There are words that are spoken as much to ourselves as to others: vows that bind us to one another and to ourselves, promises, confessions.

Beyond any account of what words do, however, there stands language itself. Language is not what is in the dictionary, though the dictionary is full of words. Language is not what we say to each other, but the air that our speech breathes. Language itself can never be seen, or said, or heard because it is a system, a dynamic, a set of possibilities waiting to unfold, waiting to be fulfilled. This aspect or that may be interrogated, described, and understood, one may talk *about* language, but always from within language itself. Language itself always outreaches any account of it.[2] The world of language is just that, a world. Language is to words, in a way, as the living world is to the particular life. Words are what they are and do what they do within language, just as a particular life is what it is only in relation to the life around it.

Human beings have experienced a deep link of world and language. Words name reality and link reality through the web of language. "We address an indissolubly languaged world and we speak an indissolubly worlded language."[3] We say the names that link things as a world, and we know by their names what they are. We say the names, and saying them gives us a place in a spoken world. The language is worlded, too. "Rain" may be an arbitrary sound to begin with, but the word becomes heavy with the rains we have known. The word carries for each of us more than the sense of rain; it carries the memory of it. The word is inseparable from the world it names, and for each of us it carries our own identity with it: I am the person to whom "rain" means what it means.

> ...Perhaps we are here in order to say: house, bridge, fountain, gate, pitcher, fruit-tree, window....
> *Here* is the time for the *sayable, here* is its homeland. Speak and bear witness.[4]

This is a fragment from Rilke again, one of the greatest poets to dwell upon the mystery of language and the life which emerges through speech. He puts the question in such a simple and radical way. Perhaps we are here in order to *say*. Saying becomes the heart of the human vocation, gathering the world up into praise, lament, prayer, offering it up as a living world realized through speaking.

Speaking a world

Humankind has no memory of how language came about among us. And who can remember learning the use of language for the first time? We learn other languages, but that's not the same. There are those who have suffered a terrible aphasia and lost the power to choose words, forgotten all the words of a lifetime and must begin to learn again. But that learning is a recovery of lost years, re-possessing the words for a world you have already known, not the opening up of a new world, not the creation of a new world.

Although we no longer remember, just as we cannot remember the creation of the world, we each had a world take shape within our imaginations, the world most immediate and real to us, through our learning and piecing together of what was addressed to us. That world expanded, changed, perhaps even was shattered and replaced in time. But the fundamental situation of being addressed, of both receiving and building a world and an identity within it, is indelibly stamped upon us as what may be called, ponderously, "the linguisticality of experience."

Look on the faces of infants and see what their faces show. See how they watch our mouths, see how they shape their mouths to fit, shape their faces to fit our faces, how they look when they nurse, what happens at the sound of a voice. The face, the voice, the sound, the shape, the touch, the milk: they aren't *about* mother; they *are* mother. They aren't *about* a world; they *are* the world. It's all Word to them. It is all creation and communication of a world. It's all testimony of how things are, and where we are.[5] Augustine reflected upon the life of the infant in which God was "crying out to [us] by means of all those senses and faculties, internal and external, which you bestow upon us."[6] Even when nursing was all we knew, Augustine urged, God spoke in the nursing. We drink Word from our mother's breasts. It's all sacrament, in a way, by which we see, feel, hear, touch, taste, and eat Word. Who knows? Perhaps that is an origin within us of the possibility of a sacramental Word, of a food that speaks, of a speaking that feeds, of a Word in flesh that gives itself into our mouths.

The communication of a world is also the communication of ourselves within the world. In listening for Word we finally heard our own names and recognized they were us. Do we carry some deep memory of hearing that one sound spoken over and over in love, of the long search to understand what this sound means only to discover that what you were hearing all those times was your own name spoken to you? I've done it myself as a father saying to our infant children, "Hello, John! Hello, Peter!" over and over with as much love as I knew how to voice, trying to coax the response, wanting nothing better than a smile and a look of recognition, trying to give love and a name in the same breath, the same word. We could say it like this: you and I learned our names listening for Word. We learned our names by discovering we were being spoken by the speaking world. Perhaps it is a secret memory of hearing this ourselves, and depending for everything upon the one who gave such a Word, which prepares in us a hunger for another Word which gives love and food and name and world.

One night our young firstborn was learning to talk and couldn't sleep. While I was walking him he leaned toward the window and pointed for me to take him there. As I held him up to see he began to call out in a tone of mixed delight and awe, "tree," "light," "car," "rain"! The words weren't just said; they were exclaimed. It was as if each word was a prayer bead made of recognition and acclamation, recited in an urgent liturgy of speaking. The holiest mystery couldn't be greeted any more wondrously and joyfully than this! As he learned to talk, as he learned the ways of signs and gestures, he was being incorporated into a shared world of names, a language-shaped world. The words were not his. The words preceded him, for this is not Adam giving names. Language was not so much something he learned as something to which he was joined. In an odd way, he did not speak, but language spoke through him, language took up his voice. Humankind gives names, but it is the flow of language that gives humankind a speakable world to live in and a place within it.

Breaking the bonds of deadly words: The preparation of freedom

The words you can say make the world you can imagine; the world you can imagine shows you what lives you can lead. How often have you met this truth? Your eleven o'clock appointment is only one example. There's the teen-age boy who can't go beyond his father's sayings of what it means to be a man. There's the man who can't go behind *his* father's sayings and has lived out his life in someone else's bitterness, taken like a small poison every day. There's the sixteen-year-old girl whose only words for herself are "fat" and "ugly," the girl who tells you she hates herself, and for whom you are afraid. There is the grandfather who loves to say the words "wickedness," and "chastisement," and "wrath of the Lord," words that you can see marked on the bodies of his family as clearly as tattoos. And this is to say nothing of the words people use, often without a sliver of reflection, to speak of the "others" near and far with whom they share the world. "War of words" is not just a figure of speech. How much of your own work as a pastor, teacher, and preacher is a battle in this war?

Speech is not only *about* the world; it makes a world, incorporates us into it, orients us within it, and speaks to us of how to speak, how to talk of our own lives and others, how to see and hear, how to live: a remarkable power. Freedom, yes, but also bondage; healing, but also harm; love and hate, hope and despair, life, death: speech is capable of all this. The power of death, wherever else it may reside, resides within the words we say. I have known women and men who died because of the words they had to carry, sometimes within them, sometimes upon them. I have seen how others have killed because of the words they had within *them*. I have listened as words at war ravaged the person who held them. I have witnessed the "unspeakable" happen because it was, in fact, quite speakable and had been spoken before. We each can name our own examples of how the power of death dwelt among us in the words we said and heard, and how they made a world where death was the answer. There is a duty, I believe, to remember by name those one can, and how it came about that words did such a thing.

Death may be the extreme, but the power of death stands behind every kind of oppression. If language is the "house of being," then it may be a "prison-house of being." The book of Hebrews speaks of humanity as those who through fear of death were subject to a life-long bondage. All fear may be understood as rooted in this fear of death, drawing strength from the threat of destruction, however disguised or displaced or transformed through the web of signs it may be.[7]

All freedom, in the same way, may be understood as rooted in a defiance of death and celebration of life. Freedom anticipates the destruction of death, refuses to live by fear, and thereby overcomes the power of death to make slavery. This, too, is the strange insistence of Hebrews, which speaks of Jesus' suffering what the "children" have suffered so that the one who held the power of death, the devil, might be destroyed (Heb. 2:14).

Such freedom, wherever else it may reside, resides among the words we say. Through speech our imagination takes its most explicit public shape. A different possibility must become speakable before it can become real to us, even if only as a hope. Aristotle concluded that poetry was finally superior to history. History was restricted to what had been, the actual; poetry spoke of the possible, what might be.[8] Through making audible a different possibility, a different future becomes thinkable. When a different future becomes thinkable, a present bondage becomes breakable. When bondage becomes breakable, there is pronounced upon it the judgment that it is not the boundary of "the way things must be" but of the "way things have been told." There is more possibility to tell than this.

Speech, then, which may be the preparation of bondage, may also be the preparation of freedom. This is Gaston Bachelard's depiction of how the poetic image speaks and works upon our imagination.[9] It may be difficult for many to hear in the word "poetry" anything capable of such a role. Poetry has so often been experienced as disconnected, fantastic, "merely" aesthetic, or precious and self-indulgent, all of which and more has been the case.

By poetry I mean speech in which what is at stake in speaking itself is put before us: what is at stake in listening, hearing, answering, naming; what is at stake in living by words, with words, through words. Think of poetry not as a specialized speech, in a specialized realm of feeling or art, but as an intensified speaking.

Think of it as words arising from, testifying to, and pointing toward what is essential, real, and possible. Like Rilke's "perhaps we are here to say," poetry may be called the speech through which our human vocation is expressed. Through hearing the Word that is addressed to us by the mystery we inhabit, and by answering as a testimony to the deep relation of things, poetry discloses who, where, and how we are, and may be. This is not so much a high claim for poetry, as a low one; such poetry is not the pinnacle of speech, but its foundation. What makes speech poetry is the quality of hearing and answering, the quality of testimony, responsibility, saying what must be said.

Re-membering

"The image has touched the depths before it stirs the surface," Bachelard wrote.[10] The surface he refers to is the realm of concepts, arguments, reason, deduction, explanation. The poetic image does not seek first, or perhaps ever, a hearing in that way. It speaks past this surface to address the imagination directly, to descend the great ocean of language which lies within us.

What are these depths the image touches? In part they are depths of memory. The word, the image, awakens a past. When the image touches depths of memory, it sets experience itself in motion: combining and recombining the elements, turning the light here, throwing this into shadow, bringing colors together with their complements, their opposite numbers on the wheel, so each shows up in full vibration. This, the image itself does. It touches the bedrock of language, pushes speech up all of its own. The connections and combinations are not made by decision, by will. When we attend to what a particular image sets ringing for us, isn't it more like this: The words seem to search out on their own the place they mean to go? Far from determining what we will hear, don't we discover where the image has gone? You can't call back an image once it has sounded within, any more than poor blind Isaac could call back his given blessing. It has been heard, and it is at work.

Memory is more than personal, however. Language itself bears memory of which its speakers are unaware. It is historical, which is to say that it carries the marks of its speakers' lives: what they have seen and heard, said and done, thought and felt. To touch the depths of memory, therefore, means reaching toward human experience broader than my own which indwells me in the very language I speak. It opens to me books of the human heart that, though already within me, had remained closed. It opens the gate to the city. I find I cannot just enter at will. I cannot simply will myself to exploration or to reverie — or perhaps to prayer or praise, for that matter, which are also matters of speech. I need the image to be a gate through which I enter the city of memory and imagination.

Shelley once observed, "Metaphorical language marks the before unapprehended relation of things." That was modified by Owen Barfield to say that metaphorical language marks the *forgotten* relations of things.[11] The image has the power to connect what had been disconnected, to restore to the center what had been left or driven to the margins. It has the power to bring into a different relationship experiences, times, places, which otherwise were held apart by the presently configured structures of memory. The image brings together horizons I cannot hold any other way. The image has the power to break down boundaries of past, present, future, what was, what is, what may be.

In this one can see that these depths we're talking about are not only depths of memory, then, but also of possibility. The image has the power to open up possibility. Where the depths are stirred and begin to move together in new and powerful ways a different future may come into view. The image "re-images." The image re-tells. The image re-names. The image re-awakens, therefore, or perhaps awakens for the first time the person who is addressed and may hear and answer *now,* and *differently.*

They had been friends for at least a dozen years. The three of them had seen each other through birth and babies, sick parents, the troubles of marriage. They had confessed thoughts and feelings they shared with no one else. No one.

Then one day the conversation seemed strained, edgy, distracted. The usual lead-ins led nowhere. Little silences appeared awkwardly and unaccountably and finally grew until the talk trailed off completely. At first no one noticed because each was thinking her own thoughts. After a while, however, all three of them were aware that no one was talking, and all three of them began to wonder what it meant. The longer no one spoke, the heavier the silence became. Did it mean something was wrong? Did it mean that there was nothing to say? Or did it mean that there was something waiting to be said and all the other words had withdrawn themselves to leave the clearing open for what was coming?

It was Karen who finally spoke. "We have never talked about God."

Barbara and Marie registered puzzlement in their faces but didn't reply.

"I just realized we have *never* talked about God." She looked from one to the other repeatedly. "Have we? Well, have we?"

"No," Barbara said, shaking her head. She looked toward Marie, who shook her head, too, "No."

Karen's gaze searched back and forth from face to face. Barbara and Marie both shifted in their chairs, not quite looking back. More silence. "*Why* don't we ever talk about God?" she asked.

Silence again.

"Maybe we're embarrassed to," Barbara said at last, color rising up her neck.

"Or don't really know how," Marie said, "I mean, to do it right." She looked down at the table. "Maybe..." but then she stopped. Her two hands slowly clasped in front of her, harder and harder, until her arms began to shake and her indrawn breath sounded ragged, catching in the back of her throat.

The poesis of life

The touching of the depths that we have termed memory and possibility the French philosopher Gaston Bachelard calls "reverberation." In this reverberation our relationship to the image changes. "The image, the poem becomes our own.... We begin to have the impression we could have created it, that we should have created it.... It expresses us by making us what it expresses."[12]

The word "poesis" means to make. But it is not so much a poet who makes poetry, as the other way around. The image has a recreative power to draw one's imagination into its special shape. It becomes part of one's identity by shaping from the inside out the life that enfolds it, so that one comes to live the image. The poetry makes one a poet, by making the hearer into someone who speaks.

This is to say that the image neither remains at a distance nor simply interior. As Robert Bly insists, it "slips suddenly inward. ...A poem is something that penetrates for an instant into the unconscious."[13] Where that does not happen no poem happens. No poem happens because nothing forgotten has been recovered, because nothing new has been glimpsed, no revolution founded. Until the image has "slipped inward" there is no basis for *understanding,* only for explanation. A poem that does reach inward, however, is the beginning of revolution because of its power to become embodied.

Adrienne Rich offers a depiction of the work of an image that is different from Bly's, one that shows a different kind of embodiment and spatiality to the process:

> Vision begins to happen in such a life
> as if a woman quietly walked away
> from the argument and jargon in a room
> and sitting down in the kitchen, began turning in her lap
> bits of yarns, calico and velvet scraps. . . . [14]

As the woman sits musing with and among the various emblems of place and time and people and herself, she pushes and pulls them according to the embodied wisdom of her hands,

> dark against bright, silk against roughness,
> pulling the tenets of a life together. . . .

discovering, rediscovering, imagining the "many-lived, unending / forms" of her reality and possibility. The image here draws together not so much hidden depths but the seemingly ordinary materials of one's ordinary life. Yet these tokens of the ordinary come together in ever-expanding patterns to reveal the ever-expanding identity of the woman who muses over them. The particulars of her life bring into question how things have been told, how the world has been told; they open the possibility of possibility.

Whether one conceives the image as working from depth to surface or surface to depth is not important. What is important is how even such distinct depictions both work upon the embodied life of the speaker and the hearer, embodied persons and embodied communities alike, and how both speak of the transformative power the poetic image can set in motion through its ability to reshape imagination and speech.

What is at stake in listening, hearing, answering, naming? What is at stake in living by words, with words, through words? "There come times," Adrienne Rich writes elsewhere in the same poem, "perhaps this is one of them, / when we must take our-selves more seriously or die...." She goes on to speak of giving oneself to silence or "a severer listening," a painful and danger-ous cleansing of dead, meaningless language in order to discover an authentic voice to tell a renewed vision. The transformation of speech and imagination, and therefore of life, begins in the "cut-ting away of an old force that held her rooted to an old ground." The power of emancipation indwells the image that touches the depths and awakens what waits there. It is in this awakening of what had been effaced that we find the preparation of freedom.[15]

If this is what poetry does, then it is a truly dangerous activity both for those who make it and those who hear it. Dangerous, too, for those who would be displaced in a re-imagined world. Some of Margaret Atwood's poems lay bare the danger of poetry precisely because of its transformative power. In her "Notes To-ward a Poem That Can Never Be Written" (dedicated to Carolyn Forché, who wrote so powerfully about El Salvador) Atwood's language is supremely bare and intense in her evocation of how dangerous those who work the power of death know poetry to be to their power, and the witness to which such poetry binds one. Of a woman imprisoned in a cement cell she writes, "She is dying because she said. / She is dying for the sake of the word."[16] There is nothing beautiful in these lines; there is no novel turn of phrase or self-consciousness of style. The poem exemplifies what it is about; it is what it says. In such a situation where everything depends upon the ability to imagine a different possibility and hold to it, Atwood shows, poetry is not a matter of cleverness or beautiful speech, as it may be in the place where her own poem is read. She images for us an "elsewhere" where what is at stake in speech is clear:

> Elsewhere, this poem is not invention.
> Elsewhere, this poem takes courage.
> Elsewhere, this poem must be written
> because the poets are already dead.

What is at stake? Life, the future, community, justice, love, hope; whatever the words are which talk about what is necessary. Speech that puts before us what is really at stake in our listening, hearing, answering, and naming of mystery, ourselves, the world, the future, so that we take it to ourselves, to our embodied and embedded lives — this is poetry. "Poetry is not a luxury," wrote Audre Lorde. "It is a vital necessity of our existence."[17] As a woman and as African American she has seen what is humanly at stake in speech and how poetry is bread *and* dreams, survival *and* flourishing. From her vantage point she has seen what I believe is at stake everywhere.

What these poets and others put before us is a "poetics of transformation." It may begin with talk of metaphors or images, which can be nothing more than literary shop-talk about the tools of the trade. It soon becomes evident, however, *why* they wrestle to understand such things. It is because of their vocation of words. They take with utmost seriousness the word-shaped world in which we live, take seriously the dynamics of speech within us and among us in this world, and acknowledge their own responsibility to do what they can with what they do best. They put before us the renewed affirmation of the vocation of words. They put before us the renewed affirmation that words can have to do with freedom, defiance of death, celebration, transformation. They say it with an urgency which itself pronounces a tacit judgment upon speech that has no such grasp of its public responsibility, its vocation, its call.

From the mystery of language to the language of mystery

To speak of the middle means to speak in certain ways that are utterly specific, and in other ways that are deeply ambiguous, even contradictory. This is, I believe, the way human beings experience their lives and describe their experience. We live in the details. I live with keys in my pocket, the smell of spice on my fingers, the sound of sirens, the black and white of a printed page, the rhythms and schedules of a household, the dark wood of a Spanish guitar. Each aspect of our lives touches us through concretely embodied detail. We live in the details, it is true, but list all the details and there remains a sense that there is more. There is more than this to one's life, and more than the "this" of any possible list to the world and life itself. There is the sense that the terms of existence, the power of it, the story of it, is both what I have known and can tell, and more than I know and can tell.

In the classic study *The Burning Fountain*, Philip Wheelwright wrote of human experience as on the verge, "on the borderland of something more." Human existence he depicted as being on a threefold threshold. It stands on a threshold of time, in a present that is always opening up and always passing away. It stands upon the threshold of the world, immersed yet also distinct, enveloped yet also apart. It stands upon the threshold of the unseen, glimpsed and yet obscured, felt but never known.[18]

The images of threshold and borderland find deep echoes in the imagination. Threshold and borderland share the quality of between-ness. They signify both within and without, known and unknown. They are fixed markers of change and transition, identity and difference, meeting and separation. (Hermes, the messenger of the gods, was the god of boundaries and boundary crossing.[19]) When experience is figured this way it is centered, we might say, on the margin. The margin or threshold is not something standing at the edge of experience but in the middle of it. Rather than seeing the fixed as central and the changing as marginal, the margin between the fixed and changing becomes the center itself. This is what characterizes experience *as* experience: the encounter between the fixed and the changing. Experience is the process of understanding anew again and again because of the encounter in the midst of life with the otherness of God, world, person, and self.[20] The world I believe I see around me, and the me I believe I know in the midst of it don't stand still. What I thought I knew becomes inadequate, and what I had not even guessed becomes necessary.

Experience figured upon threshold or borderland, therefore, has the persistent mystery of between-ness at its very feet. I do not say *a* mystery, as if there were a riddle or a question that has a secret answer. It is not *a* mystery one can speak *about,* really, not something one could point to, encompass, and characterize. The always-already-in-the-midst-of quality of one's life is forever eluding description or characterization. There is no standpoint outside of experience from which to see it entire, distantly, objectively (that is, like an object I might hold in my hand and examine). In the same way, there is no standpoint outside of mystery and interpretation. Experience, mystery, and interpretation are constantly leading toward and through one another, occasioning one another, confronting one another, transforming one another.

This double sense of being founded upon a reality, immersed in it, yet being unable to encompass it and bring it to adequate expression is central to the braiding of mystery, experience, and interpretation. One of Rilke's poems evokes something of this sense:

> Whoever you are: some evening take a step
> out of your house, which you know so well.
> Enormous space is near, your house lies where it begins,
>   whoever you are.
> Your eyes find it hard to tear themselves
> from the sloping threshold, but with your eyes
> slowly, slowly, lift one black tree
> up, so it stands against the sky: skinny, alone.
> With that you have made the world. The world is immense
> and like a word that is still growing in the silence.... [21]

"Enormous space is near, your house lies where it begins, / whoever you are." Rilke's lines are full of the sense of both the immediacy of such things as house, threshold, tree, but also the vastness of sky, world, silence, unencompassable space. In the image of the one black tree lifted by your eyes into the frame of the sky the immediacy and vastness come together, so that they display each other.[22] Through the meeting of the tree and the sky both the singularity of the tree and immensity of the sky become visible as belonging to one another. This is how the world is made, the poem affirms, a world that fills empty space the way a word fills silence. Tree and world become visible together, but "whoever you are" also becomes visible: belonging with them, beholding, on the threshold of mystery.[23]

There are philosophical vocabularies to speak of such things, but they have a way of turning one from the very experience one is trying to understand. Better to use more humane words, better to speak simply of life or world or reality and understand that even such "modest" and "unsophisticated" terms are already beyond us. The life in which interpretation takes place is forever unfolding beyond my grasp in ways I enact but do not recognize. By the same token, dimensions of that life, dimensions of mystery, are constantly being disclosed to me in the dialogue of the world where the drama of a life is enacted.[24] One's life is constantly emerging through the engagements and relationships which are its substance for us: with the creation in which we walk, with the human communities and individuals who live in us and we in them, with the signs and words by which we offer life up to one another. But it is also emerging through the encounters by which our imagined worlds break down and break open.

Interpretation begins in the middle, we have said, with its dimensions of self-understanding: identity, dialogue, relationship, situation, body, history, the other, responsibility, language, and mystery. We could say, however, that it not only begins in the middle, but is intrinsically at home there. The "Between" is a term we encounter in Buber and others as the place of meeting. The Between belongs neither to the I nor the Thou, but is the space where by their meeting they become who they are. While the configuration of I and Thou is not sufficient for describing the relationship of interpreter and text, the between of interpretation may be spoken of in similar ways. The between of interpretation is a "region of unpredictable events and untheorizable practices that can never be conceptually reduced."[25] The between, the margin, the threshold, the boundary are interpretation's homeland. If the life of interpretation is to be, indeed, a spiritual discipline, then it must be a discipline appropriate to this reality: a spiritual discipline of the Between.

It may seem an odd thing to say what one means by "mystery." Isn't mystery precisely what cannot be defined, what resists understanding and explanation? Yet not everything resistant and indefinite has the quality of mystery to it. There can be riddles, puzzles, problems to solve which are simply curiosities, temporary occasions of the knowable unknown. Supply an answer and they disappear. Mystery suggests an experience of a different order, an experience that is not displaceable by any amount of information; indeed, it suggests an experience that rather than being dissipated by knowledge is intensified and deepened. To think about mystery in this sense is not the enemy of mystery but part of its contemplation.

One way to think about mystery is as the "power of the whole," to borrow David Tracy's phrase.[26] The phrase can be especially helpful because it offers a way to think of mystery, the world, and experience without dividing them into opposing regions of sacred and profane. The whole figures an inclusiveness that challenges us to keep *moving* on the path of experience, interpretation, and understanding. But for others in this time, talk of the whole is deservedly suspect. It is seen as inevitably leading back to an architecture of totality (in the way we saw Levinas use the term), with its hierarchical ways and power of over-writing or erasure of the different by the same. The whole is seen as a concept that serves the power of domination.

I believe we can speak of the whole in such a way that it emphasizes and guards the importance of difference and relationship (which will come as no surprise given the preceding pages), and it is through the interaction of these that I understand the power of the whole. By whole I mean *the relationality through which everything becomes distinctly what it is (and not something else) and by virtue of which everything in its distinctiveness co-inheres.* The whole in this sense is not the sum of the parts reduced to a single name; it is a name for how the parts are in relation to one another. It is the power of the whole that both distinguishes and binds together. Not simply and singly the power that binds, but the power that creates and holds difference in relationship.

To speak of mystery is in some ways to speak of a limit and in some ways a source. What is frequently called "limit-language" is concerned typically with boundary situations through which we recognize the limit of our existence. That may be apprehended on the one hand as a truth about one's existence, and an encounter with the furthest reach of a life. It may also be apprehended as an encounter with what stands at the limit. So to speak of mystery may be to speak either about the character of my own life (and life itself) or to speak of what surrounds and encounters my life. Calling the limits "mystery" forbids any finality to what we say the life we live is or what stands at its boundary, at its goal. No description or characterization is finally adequate, so every attempt to circumscribe (literally, to write around or draw around) meets the unconquerable resistance of mystery.

But by mystery I mean to point to source as well as limit. It is mystery as source which founds us, engages us in the midst of life, draws out response upon response into the work and play of naming, shaping, celebrating, explaining, questioning, lamenting, recounting, performing the life we *are* and the life we hope we *shall be.* "Are" and "shall be," please notice; not have or lead or get or find, as if it were somehow possible to separate me from my life and still be me, or possible to speak of my life as I do of possessions I might someday wish to own.

Sometimes the language of mystery seems to point in one direction only: from, toward; inward, outward; above, below; there, here; individual, communal; the one, the many; spirit, body; speech, silence; presence, absence. Those spiritual traditions that may be called kataphatic gather their courage together and attempt to speak of mystery in a way that hopes (however it may happen) to present or unfold some dimension of what one speaks about. Sometimes there seems even to be a confidence that by wisdom or revelation we may know and communicate truly (if not finally) about/with/in mystery. Those spiritual traditions that may be called apophatic gather their courage together and attempt *not* to speak. Resting in the unsayable, the beyond-the-sayable, requires its own hope and confidence in the way one has chosen, and in what one believes lies along or ahead on that way. Those traditions that may be called dialectical (or negative) move constantly from a saying to an unsaying by which every speech about mystery masks and distorts as it discloses, and yet discloses even as it masks and distorts. This, too, requires a confidence and hope, although only through a despair in itself that draws one constantly forward.

These traditions may stand in stark contrast with one another as to the intentions and meanings of their language (or refusal of it). What these paths share, however, is the conviction that there is something to be spoken (however directly, indirectly, or dialectically) or to keep in silence *about:* even if it is known only in the shape of a hope or longing, even if it is never to be or cannot be known, even if it finally can be indicated only as *the wholly other who always is to come.*[27] My particular journey has led me along the more dialectical ways, which has meant that my answers are always turning into my questions. What I cannot avoid is how I am continually drawn toward the places where the limit and the source meet, no and yes, difference and relation, and how the particularity of those times and places opens onto mystery yet they remain indissolubly themselves: from, toward; inward, outward; above, below; there, here; individual, communal; one, two, three, all; spirit, body; speech, silence; presence, absence. My knowledge of joy is bound to my knowledge of sorrow. My understanding of birth is bound to my understanding of death, and gratitude to loss, companionship to loneliness, the feast of the Word to the famine of the Word, the resurrection of Jesus to the crucifixion of Jesus.

We must be very cautious, let us confess, in any attempt to speak of broad human experience. This is especially true when we address understanding of what may be called religion. It is more than an intellectual caution. The misrepresentation of such a foundational dimension of people's lives has very real consequences for very real people. Historically, we must remember, such attempts have even meant for many a very real death at the hands of those with the very real power of naming. The theme of the deadly (but potentially emancipatory) power of naming has been fundamental to virtually every theology of liberation. Yet on a scale rather more intimate than history, however, perhaps you have also experienced from one side or another, what it means to be unable to communicate because both the lived life and the available words have been so different. Perhaps you have known what it is to have your own experience denied and erased through the power of misrepresentation.

Although the problems and difficulties are well known (or if not known, then acknowledged) it is necessary for a ministry of interpretation to be grounded in at least a provisional account of certain aspects of human experience in general, even if only in order to speak of the particularities of Christian interpretations and responses to such experience and, indeed, the experience of interpretation itself. It is through attempts to name both how we are different from one another *and* how we share a common life that mutual understanding is won. If we are to interpret within the community of difference, we must risk speaking of human life across seemingly impassable boundaries, even with the real possibility of our own failure, embarrassment, and need for correction. This is most urgently so when we turn to the expressions through which our most profound experiences and deepest sense of life are spoken. Then I may be able to understand what the three women really shared at their table, and what the young man saw as he gazed at the wall.

The mystery of God

Talk of mystery and talk of God are neither necessarily the same nor necessarily different. Either may be a way of avoiding the other, both for good reason and bad. Either may be authentic, either may be faithful, either may be empty or meaningless. I may speak of mystery equally out of embarrassment to speak of God and confess, or out of reticence and reverence for the Name. I may speak of God out of a desire to run from the depth and wonder of mystery and still pretend to have said something profound and mysterious. I may speak of mystery because it is vague and indefinable, never says "No" and "Yes," never pronounces judgment or forgiveness. I may speak of God in order to claim authority for what I say, a sign of how unreal my words are of themselves.

But I may also speak of God because in the stories I know best mystery offers and asks to be called upon in just such a way, and to call requires a name. And I may speak of mystery because in those same stories it is utterly clear that no name is enough, and each name must be followed by another as a kind of confession and a kind of amends. I may speak of God because that is the only way I can tell mystery into story, which is the way I understand my own life and the life of the world.

This is how the Bible speaks of God chiefly. First and last it is in a story, as a story, through a story, because of a story that God is named. This alone, even in the absence of other more material reasons, would be reason enough to affirm the dimension of experience as the sphere of revelation. "The naming of God is thus first of all a narrative naming."[28] It is a confession in response to events and the linking of events into a history. This is history in a peculiar sense, to be sure, different from so-called objective forms of history. But it is equally different from what may be called a simply subjective kind of history. In the Bible, the story is not recounted as something in the control of the community; it is not simply a story that the community may deploy as it will. Rather, it is the community that must struggle to understand itself in terms of the story that is always contesting their identity, and exceeding them by its complexity, ambiguity, and excess of meaning. It is, indeed, a *confession* in the form of a story, a confession that claims a disclosure and meaning in the realm of experience. As a confession this story testifies to what may be called revelation, that is, an unveiling of meaning in such a way that other events and meaning receive their significance from it.[29]

The Bible, however, by no means speaks *only* in story, perhaps for this very reason, as we will ponder later. Hence the other forms of confession, such as prophecy, prayer, wisdom, law, hymnody, liturgy, parable, apocalypse, liturgy. These, too, each in their particular way, testify to disclosure and the unfolding patterns of meaning founded in the founding story. They respond from the contexts of continuing narration and meaning, and thereby disclose yet more of the story's story. Thus the founding story is transformed by its history, inscribed in the rich plurality of testimony that responds to the Unnamable Name, that always exceeds what we have said.

It is chiefly through the Bible and in the church that I have found words to speak of mystery in ways that draw life together rather than pull it apart. It is mystery that presses me to speak, but what can I say that isn't just another "tale told by an idiot, full of sound and fury, signifying nothing" (to borrow from Shakespeare)? It is by saying "Creation," "Jesus," "table," "cross," "body," "justice," "love," "sister," "brother" that I find the words to speak of God, world, and humanity. In the same way, speaking with these words presses me to point *through* these signs where mystery's mark is inscribed, toward experience where the power of the whole discloses itself and hides itself. As Ebeling has insisted, "The primary phenomenon in the realm of understanding is not understanding *of* language, but understanding *through* language."[30]

I have learned how God spoke to Moses and commanded Moses, but refused to give a name, refused any fixed address, refused any image because God dwells in thick-dark mystery. I have learned how God passed by Moses in the cleft, but the glory of mystery was all Moses could see. I have learned how the Jews refused to say the name of God except once a year with no one else to hear. I have learned how the rabbis were right to tell stories of God which no one could mistake as matters simply of true and false, but stories which spoke rather of what was real and living. I understand why Paul, confronted with mystery, had to exclaim, "O the depth of the riches and wisdom and knowledge of God!" (Rom. 11:33). When the same Paul, standing right out at the rim of speech, at the farthest reach of talk about life, death, angels, governments, history — "or anything else," as his list so poignantly concludes — when this same Paul insists that stretched endlessly beyond even this is the heart which holds us and speaks of us and says Yes, I understand why he must say "God." When Jesus says, "Those who want to save their life will lose it, and those who lose their life for my sake, and for the sake of the gospel, will save it," I am confronted by fundamental mystery in what he has said. When Jesus says, "Inasmuch as you have done this for the least of these my brothers and sisters, you have done it for me," the same mystery is there. And in the great paradox that grounds the Christian gospel, the fullness of mystery is found not at the rim, at the limits of life, not in ineffability, but in the middle, where the cross of Jesus is.

To speak of mystery in the middle, then, means turning aside from talk about disembodied spiritual realms safe from the passion and flux of existence. It means to turn instead to ways and times in the life we share, in all its pain and possibility and promise, when mystery speaks itself to us and through us, so that we know what we have been given, and what we must do.[31] This speaking I take to be always partial and provisional, always particular, always about here and now, you and me.[32]

The question at hand is interpretation for preaching. Wherever else the question comes from, it comes from *here,* in the middle. The "here" it comes from is the place and time of the preacher, the situation of the preacher, the story of the preacher, the hope and wound and desire of the preacher. Wherever else the reflections and responses to the questions we take up in these pages aim, they are aimed *there,* where women and men and children are, who gather in community in the hope that there is a Word for them: there, where a preacher must read and speak.

Word and God

Interpretation is situated in the middle of language and speech, we have said. It is among words that we work, with words that we struggle, and through words that we try to be faithful to the gospel and the people. If it is to be a spiritual praxis, it must be so among words. For the preacher there is a special urgency to questions of language and speech. Our heritage speaks of something called the Word of God. What one means by Word of God, what it does, where it is to be found or heard, how it is related to our

words and actions — these are important questions, over the formulation of which our various traditions delight to disagree. But
the formulation of doctrine is one thing, and the daily struggle
and search is another. Sometimes the doctrine comes to our aid,
and helps us to hear, discern, and order what we are hearing;
sometimes it makes us deaf to what is speaking all around us.

"Word of God" links the experience of mystery and the experience of communication. We do not say, however, "the *language*
of God," or "the *syllables* of God." The Word of God as Word
refers to the *address* of God, the speaking of God. To say that it is
Word means that it takes place within the realm of language but
isn't synonymous with language or any particular part of language. It indeed *takes place*. There is an eventful quality to it,
a quality of communication.[33] The testimony of Israel and the
church to what was experienced as the Word of God is rich and
varied. In our traditions God has spoken and speaks. We speak of
God's Word heard through the speech of prophets and apostles,
in dreams and visions, in the words of sacred writings. We speak
of the Word in story, law, song, event, parable, oracle, wisdom,
prayer, and more. The scriptures figure the Word through still
other metaphors, metaphors for metaphors: honey, light, food,
seed, rain, storm, milk. In our traditions it is by Word that God
creates, sustains, guides, blesses, and saves. It is by Word and as
Word that God gives Godself to humankind; by Word God is
God to us.

In the Christian scriptures all this is pushed to the limit: the
Word becomes flesh and dwells among us. Instead of a gap between word and world, instead of a distance that always remains
fixed between the two, the church speaks of an embodied word,
an en-worded body. In the realm of language this is the greatest
and most radical movement possible. It is also the most alarming. It is alarming because it claims the possibility, even if only in
a single and unrepeatable instance, of the presence in speech of

what is spoken about. By telling a story in which word becomes flesh every story of language is judged.

This sort of reflection has cosmic proportions, however, which can hide what is more immediately at stake. What may be more alarming than the ancient story about the Word becoming flesh is this: the possibility that this same Word of God has to do with what may happen when we read the Bible, and when we communicate with one another. Who has not heard speech that was terrible and destructive? Who has not heard speech that was lifeless and empty of help? And who has not seen what else words *can* do? Who has not seen the power of words at work within us and among us? Who has not been amazed at what can happen when one person speaks to another? And this is the work of speech itself. These are our ordinary words, human words. The church puts before us the possibility that there is more than an ancient story to tell about how *once* Word became flesh. It puts before us the possibility that words and Word may and can indwell each other. Ordinary human speech can be for us the Word of God; the Word of God can be for us ordinary human speech. What can this mean?

"God is festering in our language," wrote Gerhard Ebeling. He was referring, on one hand, to the seeming triumph of secularism and atheism, and the difficulty for the contemporary person to speak of God responsibly. He was also speaking, on the other hand, of the thoughtless (and therefore irresponsible) repetition of the speech of other times whereby "God" had become equally meaningless. His graphic image of a festering in our language speaks of a wound and an infection. Rather than being addressed and tended, he saw a wound bandaged over and left hidden. But "language is the body of our spirit,"[34] Ebeling warned, and by this festering of irresponsible silence and irresponsible speech "we threaten to die of language poisoning." I do not suppose that Ebeling's warning was only for that time. It was, indeed, for that time in a particular way, but it may be voiced with equal concern now, although the particular signs and symptoms of the wound may be different.

There is now no lack of those for whom talk of God is utterly irrelevant to their actual life in the world. They keep silence about God because there is no reason to speak, nothing to be said that would effect or change anything, nothing that happens in any connection with the word "God." There is also no lack of those for whom talk of God is completely free of difficulty. They have only to repeat what has been said by others, point to the Bible, repeat the lyrics of some well-produced recorded music, or promulgate a set of propositions about the identity of God, and suppose that because they have pronounced the word "God" something of importance has been said, and something has happened. Yet "speech about God does not rule out godlessness: it can itself be abysmally godless. And contrariwise, silence about God is not in itself a sure mark of godlessness."[35] This is both a warning about the human situation as such and a warning about an unrepeatable moment of crisis in our life. Surely it is a warning about the preaching we do, and all the many and various ways we speak of God. What is the warning?

God and truth

There is something of which we do not speak that is killing us because of how we don't speak of it. It threatens the whole human body. While those who are most vulnerable suffer from this silence first, the fever is from head to foot. There is something of which we *do* speak that is killing us, because of how we speak of it. While those who are most vulnerable suffer from this talk first, the fever is from head to foot, because we are one body, we live one life.

Ultimately, what is festering in our language is the truth. To speak of God is to make a claim about the truth. To call upon the name "God" in our speaking is to testify an intention to tell the truth as completely as we can. It is (truly or falsely) an attestation of the seriousness of our intent. In the realm of language truth is an ultimate term by which we try to indicate ultimate matters, just as the word "God" indicates ultimate matters.

In some ways, God language seeks to tell truth about our own experience. Not just any experience, of course, but experience of the power of the whole that concerns a person in the most fundamental ways.[36] It is a language of response, an expressive language of relationship. It indicates our relationship to the power of the whole as one of *peace*, let us say, when it is a source of confidence to us. Alternately, in the face of meaninglessness or emptiness it may be *despair*. *Gratitude* is a response to an experience of gift, *lament* a response to hurt. In the face of the sense of effective power, order, or law it may be a language of *awe*. As a response to the apprehension of glory or radiance is the expressive language of *wonder*. As a response to the overflowing of energy or power is the language of *joy*. We could speak also of *terror* in face of what is experienced as chaos, things falling apart with nothing to hold them together, or *dread* in the face of a future that approaches in judgment. Apprehending the future as full of promise or salvation shapes the language of *hope*. *Abandonment* expresses the fundamental experience of loss, absence. *Love*, let us say, responds to the experience of grace.[37]

If God language is how we speak of these dimensions of experience which are both full of mystery and fundamentally, ultimately important to us, it also makes a public claim. It makes a public claim that these are indeed responses to the truth that concerns us all, and that by speaking of God — by preaching — one intends to testify to the truth, and therefore be held accountable. To hold together God and truth is to insist that what is at stake is fundamental and ultimate. It is to insist, at the same time, that all one can do is testify, and not demonstrate, because the truth of the truth, the truth of God, precisely because it is fundamental and ultimate exceeds us. To speak of God and truth so that they cannot be separated is to insist that we are speaking both about the actual life that we face *and* the mystery of whole. Rather than avoiding either actual existence or the power of the whole, speaking of the truth of God locates us accountably in the middle of both. It speaks of the truth that is so bound to God that it cannot be separated and still be truth, or God be God — or the speaker be the speaker.

The truth of God is not limited to any cultic speech or vocabulary (*ours* or *theirs*). It is equally at home and equally difficult everywhere. Preaching knows no native language and all languages, as Pentecost reminds us. Speaking of the truth of God, therefore, is *not* somehow speaking of a special truth that applies to a special realm and that is sayable only in a special language, to be understood by those with special training, and communicated to those with a special status, for whom it promises some special future. In the same way, to call attention to the Word of God is *not* to indicate some kind of super-speech or super-action, essentially different from ordinary speech and action, with a special power derived from a special source, power that is arbitrarily here then gone according to some secret will, and requires some special preparation in the hearer to be worthy and able to hear. The Word of God means, rather, "a true, proper, and finally valid Word."[38]

To believe the Word

To speak of God in this way means a telling of the truth by which and through which a person takes responsibility for what is said before the face of the other. "God can only be spoken of appropriately in personal commitment," insisted Ebeling.[39] This happens by the testimony of a witness who thereby commits himself or herself in accountability both for what is said and the one to whom it is said. The Word of God means communication that depends upon God and entrusts itself to God by and in speaking. Because God is not within our power to dispose or conjure, because God is not given to us to know as God under the conditions of existence, indeed, because the very servant whose ear has been awakened walks in the darkness and must rely upon the Name, the Word of God is a word of entrustment. "For since to speak about God concerns and includes the one who undertakes to do it, its truth is of such a kind that the speaker must commit [himself or herself] in [his or her] own reality, for the reality of God."[40]

The event of the Word encompasses both the speaking and the response. To be more clear, if a bit more awkward, we could say it this way: Word and faith are two different aspects of the same event. The same is true of Word and hope, and Word and love. They are *together* aspects of the same event, so that faith, hope, and love may be distinguished but not be separated in any fundamental way without essentially changing them. Thus, faith without hope and love is no longer the faith of which the gospel speaks, nor is love without faith and hope, nor hope without faith and love.

To respond could be called to "believe," if we understand that in the older English sense of the word. The roots of the word include the sense of trust, reliance, love, and loyalty.[41] It is a complex word, much richer than anything as limited as "beliefs" in the sense of opinions or views. It combines dimensions of mind, heart, action, and promise. The older usage of believing *on* captures some of the dynamic. Perhaps it is better to speak of believ*ing,* rather than belief, to keep some of that audible. If we could call the response to the Word believing then believing is what faith, hope, and love are together. When believing is turned toward God it is called faith. When it is turned toward the future, it is called hope. When believing is turned toward the other person it is called love. As a whole event, an event of communication, the speaking *and* the believing together are the event of the Word. It is not a speaking *about,* but the communication *of.* Not speaking *about* faith, hope, and love, but the communication of them. The communication of the Word of God, therefore, means the communication of faith, by faith, through faith, of hope, by hope, through hope, of love, by love, through love. Preaching is a form of faith, hope, and love enacted and made real between speaker and hearers. Preaching is believing.

As a concrete communication, the Word of God means a word that is timely, about the actual situation in which we find ourselves, that is, a proper word (in Ebeling's sense). The Word of God means a word that seeks validation in the realm of life and history and cannot rest with any validation that would abstract itself from the ongoing life of the community that trusts it. It is a word that stands ready to give an account of itself, in its thinking, as well as in its faith, hope, and love.

It insists, therefore, upon speaking of the past as a real past that bears real weight and deals with us even (and especially) when we will not deal with it, a past infinitely more complex than any telling can encompass, a past that is infinitely more sad and difficult, and infinitely more full of alternatives and possibilities than the stories invented to justify and control the present. The past, too, has been a time of testimony, and a cloud of witnesses have heard and spoken and communicated the truth by their own ordinary speech and ordinary (yet even so, extraordinary) life. It is by virtue of the past, and through the particular histories of the past, that the person-to-person speech that has communicated faith as far as here and now has come.[42]

As a true, proper, and finally valid Word, the Word of God must speak about the future. This is not just any future, to be sure, but the future of redemption: the future for which creation itself groans, which God promises through the law and the prophets, and which the church sees figured in the crucifixion and resurrection of Jesus and the breaking down of the dividing wall of hostility in the gathering of the beloved community.

As a true, proper, and finally valid Word, the Word of God comes to speak about the present, then, and to call attention to the present as the time to listen, hear, believe, speak, and act out of the truth. As the present it is the time of faith (which means nothing more than trusting oneself to the truth). The founding of the truth precedes us and it reaches us through the testimony of its witnesses. The ultimate fruition of the truth summons us especially in the conversion of our imagination and speech, and already flowers in the first fruits of hope and love. The present, then, is the time of *our* witness, the witness of those who speak as those who have heard, for the sake of those who themselves are summoned to speak. This is, indeed, what witness is: the testimony of those who are summoned to speak in a dispute about the truth. Isn't this what you hope to do when you enter the pulpit? Somehow, by the grace of God, to tell the truth?

By the grace of God: as a word of faith, hope and love, the truth of the Word of God depends upon the truth of God for its validity, and for its being heard as valid. Ultimately it is neither sufficiently wise of its own, nor sufficiently powerful of its own; it is foolish and weak because it is ultimately bound to the folly and weakness of the cross. It stakes itself on the scandal and offense of the crucified one, who is utterly indistinguishable to religion or philosophy or law as anything other than a transgressor of all three. It stakes itself on the scandal and offense of the crucified one, who is indistinguishable to cultural, national, and political identity as anything other than an outsider and stranger. It stakes itself upon a claim of truth that this is the very place God is to be met, and from which God enters without reserve into the heart of human life, so that there is no more anywhere upon the earth or under the earth from which the promise of God can be excluded. Even death is no longer able to determine humankind, as captivity itself is led captive to the word of life and freedom. In both the simplest and most complex sense, the Word of God is the communication, stronger than death, *of* faith, *by* faith, for the *sake* of faith; *of* hope, *by* hope, for the *sake* of hope; *of* love, *by* love, for the *sake* of love.

Because the dispute about the truth is met across the whole horizon of our speech, testimony must reach across the whole horizon, as well, in all the forms of our speaking. The world of reality is at stake; therefore we must respond with the fullest truth of which we are capable.

Listening for the Word

It is late in the day now. Upon the desk the Bible is open to the same page it was in the morning. The paper is very thin and makes a lisping sound when it is turned. If you press down you can see letters printed on the other side. There are more markings beside certain verses than there were yesterday. Your own words are written in the Book. Words among words among words, coming forward, fading away like the moments of a day do, leading into one another, leading away sometimes, many voices. The day's journey has been a journey among words, from text to text to text. It has been a search among words, or a waiting among words, for something one could call the Word of God.

The Gospel of Mark tells how Jesus once went down to the Jordan, a pilgrim among pilgrims, to be baptized by John. The skies opened overhead, the story says, a bird dove in the air, and a voice spoke to him and said, "You are my beloved child, with you I am well pleased." I have never heard such a thing. God has never spoken to me aloud, nor to anyone I know.

How would you recognize the Word? Do we know it when we hear it? Or do we recognize it later, just as the two disciples at the table in Emmaus recognized Jesus only as he vanished, and remembered how the stranger's words had moved them? Can we point to a word printed on a page and say "here"? Can we point to scribbling on the pad and say "there"? Is it the word that woman was saying this morning, or that passed between those three people at the café? Is it something always behind us and always up ahead?

Rather than offering a definition, the primary language of the faith directs our listening toward where the Word *may* be heard because it *has* been heard before.[43] The Word has to do with the words we read on the page of scripture. The Word has to do with our words and actions at the table and the font. The Word has to do with listening, preaching, and hearing. The Word has to do with the gathered community and what we do together. The Word has to do with the embodiment called incarnation, and the body called church. The Word has to do with telling the truth. The Word has to do with the neighbor, the stranger, and the enemy. The Word has to do with the face of the other. The Word has to do with receiving a name, and a world, and a future. The Word has to do with the Name one must hear in the dark, and which will bear your weight in the dark. The Word which convicts and releases, which judges and forgives, binds and looses, wounds and heals, singles out and brings together, the Word which makes freedom and authors faith is intimately bound to the words we say and write, read and hear, witness and enact.

Luther taught that understanding of the scripture is a continual movement that can never be exhausted. It is continually under the threat of turning living understanding into dead letter unless it is renewed and discovered afresh. "For what one already possesses is always the letter, by comparison with what has to be achieved."[44] As Ebeling explains, "The Spirit turns into the letter; but the letter must in its turn constantly become the Spirit once again. One stage of understanding is always the letter from which the Spirit comes in the next stage."[45] A radical statement. If Luther is right, and I believe he is, then this is true of all the ways Word comes to us. We cannot say in advance how the Word will be spoken. We cannot say in advance what the Word will do. "I shall be who I shall be." "Behold I am doing a new thing; even now it breaks forth from the bud. Can you perceive it?" Yet even if this Word cannot be captured, encompassed, and defined, the church proclaims that if it is the Word of God we are hearing it will be a word of mercy and justice, it will be a word of faithfulness, hopefulness, and love, and it will point a way for us to walk humbly upon earth.

Interpretation lives in daily confrontation with the power and mystery of language. There is no choice about that. There are choices about *how* we live in that confrontation. We can choose how to attend on a given day to what is speaking all around and within us. We can choose to search out certain voices and turn away from others. We can direct our feet down certain streets and await what may be heard there. What will come to our ears we cannot say. What we *can* say is how we shall try to listen for the Word among the words.

Listening is where speech is born that is true to the life that surrounds us. Listening is where speech is born that is essential, foundational. Listening is where speech is born that is bread and dreams; where speech is born that grasps what is at stake where one person speaks to another: life, the future, community, justice, love, hope. Listening is where speech is born which can be the preparation of freedom. Listening is where speech is born which can in its own turn become among us the Word of God.

Open my ear to listen as one who is taught, O God.

Four

Scripture as Scripture

The Book ✦ Writing, not speaking ✦ Scripture and sacredness ✦ Revelation ✦ Ways of knowing ✦ A storied world ✦ Knowing by doing ✦ Call, re-calling, re-membering, standing in the place of truth ✦ Speaking in parables ✦ Wisdom ✦ Hymning and healing ✦ Gates to the city

Morning by morning by morning by morning. The Bible waits where you left it. On the bookshelf sit other translations, but the book on the desk is the one you think of as "your" Bible. It is not just a matter of translation, of course, but relationship. We each have a history of Bibles we have known.

My grandmother's sitting room had an enormous Bible on display, old, worn, and as severe in its appearance as the faces of the fading family pictures that surrounded it. The words "Holy Scripture" were seemingly carved in the cover, and shone with gold. It appeared to me as a child that the shelf was a kind of throne from which, in the form of this enormous book, God watched.

In church on Sunday another Bible, even bigger, rested upon the communion table. It too sat upon a stand, slightly tilted forward, open, with a large red ribbon angled across the page. Yet another Bible rested upon the lectern, from which the minister would read. After the end of the lesson the Bible was lifted up: "The Word of the Lord." "Thanks be to God," we replied.

A small pocket testament is held in the hands of an old veteran, a veteran testament returned from the war. Tracts of the Gospel of Mark are passed round a circle of migrant workers; one person reads, others listen. A line of teenagers stands in front of a congregation. It is their day to recite the verses they have chosen, make public promises they only dimly understand, and receive a Bible with their own names embossed on the cover. On the street corner, a preacher holds a megaphone to his mouth with his left hand, and raises a Bible high in his right, like flag. Beside a hospital bed a young mother strokes the forehead of her unconscious child and holds a Bible to her own heart. In a crowded auditorium an evangelist paces back and forth across the stage, thrusting a Bible toward the audience as if lightning might fly from the book and consummate the judgment of God. Alone in a hotel room a man looks at himself in the mirror, empties a bottle down the sink, pulls open the night stand, and takes out the Bible he knows he'll find there. He opens it and puts his finger down on the first page he sees.

The Book

"Words, like waves, break on the shore," he said, "but what we decipher is always a bit of foam."   — Jabès[1]

Every word is first of all the echo of a lost word.   — Jabès[2]

The book is as old as water and fire. Reb Rafan.   — Jabès[3]

The Book is open upon the desk.[4] The movements by which it has come to be there are automatic; stop and try to remember them and you may not be able to, you have been this way so many times before. Your body knows this book. The weight, the texture of the cover, the feel of the binding cupped in the curve of your hand, the feel of the paper beneath your finger. But also the smell of it, and the sounds of opening, closing, the lisp of the page turning.

You have shaped yourself to this Book. In order to read you have composed yourself, and hour upon hour your body has revolved around it. Leaning forward, pushing back, a rocking motion, a cradling in your lap, a peering, a shaking of your head, a cramp, the muscles around your eyes which tighten in a frown, the same muscles which stretch to smile, the chin resting upon the hand, the elbow resting upon the desk. Your body knows about the Book, this silent partner that promises nothing, asks nothing, and responds to nothing — and, of course, which promises, asks, and responds to everything. If you were to see yourself reading, what would you see? Something like a walk, perhaps, an embrace, a wrestle, a dance, the movements of a liturgy?

This is an intimate knowledge, and like every intimate knowledge it is marked by ceremony and ritual. And as with every authentic ceremony and ritual, the heart of it lies in what we enact beneath our awareness; not where we perform the rite, but where the rite performs us; not the meaning we bring to it, but the meaning which the rite gives to us who enact it.

It is an irony that the more we recognize and understand what we do and why, the deeper the heart of our actions withdraws. The more it withdraws the deeper one is drawn after. By understanding I come to the edge of my understanding of these things that I do, only to find that I must reach out from there now. The real ritual and ceremony begin past the last grasp of our reach, but only just past, maybe even close enough to be touched by the ends of our fingers, but not held. The real ritual and ceremony lie in what we do not yet recognize we are doing, because we are actually doing it, knowing it in our bodies, not explaining. The proper goal of a liturgy is to be transformed into the most immediate acts of a day, so that we know them no longer as liturgy, but as the way we live.

So it is with the ceremony and ritual of reading. Learn to read, and everything you learn signals ever more clearly that reading really will begin the next time you open the Book, for which all the reading until now has prepared you. The Book also continually withdraws in the same way that our liturgies do: drawing you forward toward the Book, which is inscribed everywhere and which you read in the same way you breathe.

As a student many years ago, I heard a teacher pronounce "the *Word*" with such intensity and wonder it was as if I was hearing it said for the first time. The shock was that he held in his hand nothing more than what I held in mine: a Bible, which was moments before a particularly excellent and important book, but for all that a book among books. Yet on that morning, in that room (it is not far from here, I pass it most days, and sit in it now as a teacher myself), it began to become strange to me. Say it this way: the book began to become the Book.

Even after so many years I struggle to explain what it means to say "the Book." It is the same difficulty as giving an account of mystery, and the two have everything to do with each other. But to speak of the Book points to special aspects of mystery. It has to do, in part, with a sense of the center, the rock. It bespeaks fixity, a stability, something that stays, endures. Anchor, cornerstone, mountain, still point, North Star, a place to stand. No matter that within it there may be storm, ruin, avalanche, vertigo, thick cloud, quicksand. The Book holds them. They are contained, safe, permanent in their impermanence; they have a place, a house not made with hands. No matter that what is within the Book takes my balance away, de-centers me, drives me out, away from any Eden called "here" into the land of wandering. Am I not "there," too? Are not all my days inscribed, even if I cannot read them?

It is written . . . it is written. Jesus, put to the test by the devil, answers, "It is written. . . . " What terrible testing by the devil, who can also say, "It is written." What a terrifying assault on the fixity of the Book, on fixity itself.

The mystery of the Book also has to do with the sense of fount, headwaters, the darkness we come from. In the Book one can read, "In the beginning..." and therefore have a place to begin again. In the Book one can read, "And God said..." and therefore have something to hear. In the Book one can read "Let us make humankind in our own image, according to our likeness..." and therefore have something to say. To speak of the Book, then, testifies to a sense of "from," a claim that there is a past that reaches this far, a history. There is a Story, not just time. And even if we can only tell stories, just as the Book tells stories, those stories are themselves held and held together by the Book. In all their improbability (indeed, impossibility), partiality, incompleteness, distortion, untruth, mistakenness, evil, godlessness, they are nevertheless held. They are remembered and taken up (how else, but by grace?). Not erased, but granted to be the past for us, even for our sake. And am I not also one who is included in this "for-our-sakeness"? Not one who is forsaken, but exactly the opposite: for-our-sakened.

To speak of the Book also means to speak of a sense of "toward." In the Book we read of an Omega, a holy city, promise transformed into fulfillment — not just *a* promise, but promise itself fulfilled. The beginning is necessary if there is to be an end, but it is the end that draws the beginning forward. It is the end that defines the beginning as the "beginning of the good news," the beginning of what still lies ahead. There is where the stories meet in all their improbability, incompleteness, and the rest, to be redeemed together with us — and how could it be redemption if the Book were not redeemed, too? How could it be the wiping away of all tears if it did not include the tears shed with, because of, and by the Book?

"The book is as old as water and fire." As old as water: the waters above and below are older than creation. They are not made, but gathered into place, divided. They are there, waiting to be filled with light, earth, life, humankind. The book old as water is the Book waiting to be written. The Book waits to become what it will be, and the spirit broods over the face of the Book.

As old as fire: take a match and put it to paper. How old is the fire burning inches from your hand? Moments ago it wasn't there, not this fire. Yet the fire *is* the same fire that has burned and will burn. Whether it flickers or roars, whether it burns as the lights in firmament above or curls around the corner of the paper, it is both ancient and newly born.

If the Book is fixity (and this is not a historical claim, but a religious one), and if Reb Rafan is right, then it is the strange fixity of water and fire. The Book is the fixity of movement, wave surge and combustion, from beginning to end, constantly consuming and consumed, constantly flowing down, out, dispersing, rising, gathering, falling.

So much of a preacher's identity is tied to a history and relationship with the scriptures. So much of the work of preaching is tied to what one's experience of scripture has been.

Some of it is undoubtedly hard history and bad relationship. You may have found yourself a target and the scriptures used to attack you and wound you. You certainly have ministered to others in that place. Even if you have been able to bring scripture to shield them from scripture you know the harm that can be (and has been) done. You have surely agonized over passages you wish to God were not there, and prayed for better answers than the ones you have for why they are.

Some of the history and relationship is wonderful and full of wonder. Moments when everything seemed to fall into place in impossible harmony. Experiences of meaning so rich and profound you didn't dare speak. Coming to such clarity that you knew you *had* to speak, and what you had to say, because the scriptures had shown you.

All these experiences and more are so much a part of a preacher's identity that to ask about one's relationship with scripture is to ask a bedrock question, indeed. So much of our daily life is tied to the reading of these scriptures that it is hard to step back and ask a simple question: What does it mean that we *read* scripture?

Writing, not speaking

In the Beginning, affirms the scripture, God spoke. In many and various ways God has spoken. In the End God will speak. We, however, do not live in the Beginning, or at these other times and places, nor at the End. "Speak to *me*," prays the hymn.

You, too, have spoken in many and various ways. You will speak again, although you do not know now what you will say, and will not know until you say it. You may, indeed, prepare words for speaking, but until the moment comes our own speech is hidden from us. One day you will speak in human speech for the last time. All the speaking will be done. Whatever was said and unsaid will remain just that way, and will continue to roll away in widening echoes: your speech presence in the world. Between what God has spoken and what you have yet to say stands the present time. In the most immediate sense that means this particular day. And within this day, it means the time in front of the scripture. "Speak to me," prays the hymn, "that I may speak."

The scripture, however, is silent. We read "Thus says the Lord, . . ." but what follows is not the voice of God but writing. We read "And Moses said, . . ." yet what follows is not the voice of Moses, but writing. We read "You have heard it said, . . . but I say unto you, . . ." yet instead of hearing speech we read writing. Open the Book and you find signs without a voice. Although one speaks of *listening* to the text, although I say, "Jesus said . . ." as if I had heard, I have not heard. I have read.

Scripture is writing, not speaking. Whatever else being scripture means, it means being written; whatever else writing represents, it represents the absence of voice. Because writing and speaking would seem to share so much, an inevitable temptation comes to put aside the differences between them — less a temptation, perhaps, than a drift — and forget how deep the difference is. Yet so much that makes interpretation what it is depends upon this difference.

Speaking belongs to the situation of presence, dialogue, address, reply, gesture, intonation. Speaking is clothed in the particulars of voice and body, the mystery of a sound emerging from a hidden space within, the mystery of it reaching into another hidden space within where neither the speaker nor hearer can see.[5] The situation of speaking is in process, open to negotiation, persuasion, change, or even reversal of meaning or roles. So we have God and Moses, Jesus and the Syro-Phonecian woman, Gamaliel and the Sanhedrin, Paul at the Areopagus. The very vitality, mystery, and dynamism of voice, however, make it fragile. The sound fades, the situation changes, the discussion moves on, partners separate and take up other speech, the speakers and hearers die. As speaking it cannot endure.

In Scripture, however, the situation is different. Words remain, but not presence, gesture, or voice. Only the words themselves, or more precisely, the signs of them in the form of mute inscriptions endure. As writing, words no longer are bound by the chain of memory and repetition. They are removed from the context of speech, gesture, voice, intention. They have broken away from the scene of author, context, and original audience. Writing possesses a kind of independence and autonomy. It doesn't even have to be read; indeed, it can lie unread for hundreds or thousands of years and still be *readable*. It is fixed, and therefore closed in a certain way. But by the very combination of being closed and closed off from the act of speech, it becomes open in a different way. Freed from the context of immediacy, presence, speaking, a particular moment in a particular place, writing becomes available in a different context to mean differently.[6] The fluidity of the signs themselves emerges, their overtones and echoes. The very indeterminacy and inadequacy of signs to say *one* thing absolutely, become not writing's defect, but its possibility to mean more and (necessarily) differently by what it means now.

Although these issues are very much with us now, they are, in fact, already thousands of years old. Rabbinic interpretations of the Torah have flowed from an understanding of *two* Torahs, one written, one oral, both given by God at Sinai. In the written Torah God has intended all and given all in a superabundance of meaning. Interpretation unfolds what is given through the processes of history and community. Midrash searches out the connections, and by the process of dialogue unites in the life and imagination of the community the hidden intentions of the text. Midrash itself becomes text in time and thus provokes the oral response of dialogue among still others, and on and on.[7] Early Christian interpreters inherited much of this understanding through the Christian scriptures themselves. They also brought understandings of speech and writing from philosophical traditions (particularly Plato) that placed truth in the first position, speech in the second, and writing in the third. Writing was seen as a lesser imitation of speech, and speech as a lesser imitation of the truth. Augustine developed a powerful theory of signs that recognized how complex language is, how difficult and limited understanding is, and how fraught with peril is the journey from one to the other. Words have meanings that go beyond the intentions of those who say them or write them, and God's intention — whether in the things of the world or the works of humankind — will always exceed us. This is as true of scripture as any other writing, because language is a human thing. When we understand at all, he insisted, it is because the Teacher has taught us.[8] Tradition has sought to address the problem of scripture's silence by means of various rules of faith, teaching offices, theological systems, church authority, and claims of divine disclosure, the need for which underscores the point. Why is interpretation necessary in the first place? Precisely because scripture is silent and cannot explain for itself what it means.

When the interpretation of writing is central to spiritual life, that means daily encounter with the reality of the silence behind the words on the page, and the staggering possibilities of connection and meaning: absence and astonishing abundance.

"I've been wanting to ask a question, pastor, but I'm kind of embarrassed."

"Embarrassed?"

"Well, I think it may be a dumb question, or maybe I should already know the answer."

The other members of the Bible study look a little hopeful, as if it might be *their* dumb question and somebody else would ask it so they wouldn't have to.

"You know the saying: 'The only dumb question is the one you don't ask.' You'll probably do everyone a favor by asking."

She looked around the group. A retired cabinetmaker, a teacher, a medical secretary, another homemaker like herself, a pharmacist, a social worker, a college student away from home. Most of them were acquaintances rather than friends. Some were longtime church members, some brand new. Some were reading the Bible for the first time (or at least since Sunday school), some were old hands at Bible study. Some were reading out of curiosity, some to save their lives.

"Okay, here goes. When I read this story (it was Jesus and the ten lepers) I see a story about being grateful. The moral is we should be grateful to God. Am I wrong?"

"No, not at all."

"But for the last half hour we've been talking about all kinds of other things like baptism and worship and confession, and so on. Don't get me wrong, I think it's great, but how did we get all the way from point A to point...Z? Where does all that come from?"

"From lots of places. From the story, from other stories, from elsewhere in the Bible, from church tradition, from people's experiences, from the news."

"But Jesus didn't say all those things to the lepers."

"No, he didn't."

"Then how do we know that what we've been talking about is what the scripture really means?"

Scripture and sacredness

What does it mean to call the Bible *scripture?* It is already a confession, perhaps not entirely intended. What is at stake in this word? That is, in fact, the very question the word itself puts to us. The word itself asks what we mean, what relationship is signified. Is *scripture* a promise, a plea, a rejection? Is it only the same as *text, writing, book?* Does scripture mean The Book? Does it mean holy or sacred?

To speak of the sacredness of the scripture is in some ways simple. There are those for whom it is not a question at all. The sacredness of the scriptures is so much a given that it is thought about only when the scriptures are attacked. For others the question is simply self-evident, as simple as saying "Law" or "Word of God." For others the question is enormously complex and conflicted. It is theological, social, linguistic, ontological, mystical, existential, hermeneutic. For others it is a meaningless question. "Holy Scripture" is the title of a book, but the Holy part of the title does not affect them and their reading in any way. Yet how the interpreter understands the sacredness of the scriptures (or the relevance of the question) shapes the experience of interpretation profoundly.

In some ways what we mean by holy or sacred (the terms are interchangeable here) is like what we mean by mystery and the power of the whole. The responses of awe or joy or dread or hope that we named can be understood as responses to the holy. Yet holiness can have certain shades of meaning that the idea of mystery doesn't. The biblical *qadosh,* for instance, communicates the sense of something set apart by God or for God. Holiness has to do with God. It belongs to God first of all, so whatever is holy or becomes holy is so by virtue of God's holiness. As God's, the holy is evoked by Rudolf Otto's classic term "the wholly other," an otherness which is not to be transgressed. The sacred serves to mark and set apart what it touches. Moses' face shines as a sign of speaking with God. A holy people is a people set apart (even if they are set apart for the sake of all the world) and carry marks of it on their bodies. So holiness has to do with identity, and identity is established by one's relation to holiness. The sacred is numinous, charged with power and glory, fascinating and dangerous, full of the potential for transformation. You take your shoes off on holy ground, you cling to the mercy seat, you enter or stay away from the tent of meeting all because they are holy, and holiness means transformative power, including the power of life and death.

The sacred also carries the sense of ultimacy or the really real, perhaps eternity. To deal with the sacred (or to be dealt with by the sacred) is to be confronted by what matters most whether we were aware of it or not. So Jacob awakens to discover that he had been sleeping on holy ground, or Thomas, face to face with the pierced and risen Jesus, exclaims, "My Lord and my God!"

Like mystery, holiness eludes our grasp, perhaps because one senses we are in the grasp of *holiness* first. Yet even if we cannot finally encompass all that holiness might mean, we can describe dimensions of it and attend to how our understandings of holiness affect what happens when we read the scriptures.

As we think about this, however, let us hold in the back of our minds these words of Paul Ricoeur: "I am frightened by this word 'sacred.' "[9] The words are a reminder that the question is genuinely dangerous: dangerous to ask, and not to ask; dangerous to answer, and not to answer. This, too, is a place where the vulnerability of life to language is exposed. This, too, is a place where violence hides, only to show itself when we are already in its power. The danger, however, cannot be avoided by silence or dismissal of the question; it can be met only through addressing the question and recognizing what is at stake.

The word "sacred" is dangerous in the same way the word "pure" is dangerous, or the word "chosen," or the word "righteous." It has a pull of violence to it. It steps back from the messiness and ambiguity of existence and claims a clarity, a quality of truthfulness, and an authority that need only to be declared. What does holiness have to do with the unholy? What does purity have to do with the impure, mixed, and adulterated? What does the chosen have to do with the rejected? What does righteousness have to do with iniquity? In all of these, and in like terms, the power of ultimate division rejects difference and justifies the total condemnation of the other. The word "sacred" becomes a death warrant.

Is this an exaggeration? From terrible great examples to terrible small examples the violence of the "sacred" has devastated us: holocausts, pogroms, enslavement, genocides, wars, all undertaken beneath some banner of sacred blood, sacred truth, sacred honor, sacred land; a child killed to beat the "devil" out of her, a young man left hanging dead in the strands of a barbed wire fence because he is gay, an immigrant set afire, all in the name of something someone called "sacred." And this is to say nothing of the ordinary social, political, economic, and psychic violence — even within the church — by those who believe themselves justified by the word "sacred," the ultimate justification. If the communities that value the word wish to be responsible, the real violence of its history must be acknowledged. I must acknowledge that the violence of the sacred is powerfully inscribed within the Bible itself. I must acknowledge that this violence has been re-enacted by those who like myself hold the scriptures sacred, and *by how* we have held them sacred. The *temptation* of the word, and our failure in the face of its test, must be confessed.

At the same time, however, it is of no help simply to make a scapegoat of one vocabulary in favor of another, as if the fault were in the words and not in ourselves. If the power of death is, indeed, at work in our language, it is so because the power of death is at work within and among us. We must, rather, attend ever more closely, listen ever more deeply, question ever more insistently. We must guard, perhaps paradoxically, the vital impurity of our words, even where they are most reverently inscribed. We must guard their incompleteness, their need for each other, the ways they point toward another and another, depend upon one another, show themselves only with one another's help. This must be done for the sake of holiness itself, which can be guarded only by being vulnerable in this way, as the cross discloses. Much is at stake, for as it goes with such a word as "the sacred," so it goes between us.

Can it be that this is something that can be seen in the Bible itself? If the violence of holiness is written there, are there also other possibilities that appear as well? Can it be that the Bible in its multiple voices and texts itself invites — perhaps even requires — many different approaches to what holiness means? Can it be that all the different kinds of texts — story, law, prophecy, wisdom, song, parable, and the rest — pose the possibility of holiness in different ways? Can it be that the holiness of the scriptures even demands a setting aside of its holiness for the very sake of its holiness?

Revelation

Break thou the bread of life, dear Lord, to me,
As thou didst break the loaves beside the sea;
Beyond the sacred page I seek thee, Lord;
My spirit pants for thee, O Living Word.
— Mary Lathbury, d. 1913

Never does the meaning of these symbols fully dismiss the materiality of the symbols which suggest it. They always preserve some unexpected capacity for renewing this meaning. Never does the spirit dismiss the letter that revealed it. Quite the opposite, the spirit awakens new possibilities of suggestion in the letter.[10]   — Emmanuel Levinas

Augustine imagines an ascent that seeks to leave the materiality of language behind. Levinas speaks of a recurrent return to the concreteness and materiality of the language, the words themselves, in the most immediate way. The "beyond the text" is bound *to* the text.

To make an analogy: understanding bread must always be by way of eating, and each bread has the power to teach us, and each eating of bread is a new possibility. Bread that has become an idea of bread is impoverished. The idea of bread is not made of what bread is made of. There is no wheat, no water, no salt, no leaven (no lack of leaven), no marks of the pan or the heat, no crumb, crust, color, aroma or taste, no nourishment. The idea of bread does not do what bread does, and therefore it does not question us about what we do. In the idea of bread it is no longer bread we encounter, with its gifts, demands, and relationships. The idea of bread does not require a decision of me to share or not to share, to receive, to refuse, to fast, to celebrate, to give, to weigh the cost of bread for the farmer, the baker, the eater. If I am asked for bread it is not an idea of bread that is requested. It is not only the possibility of renewed imagination that the actual bread provokes, but the ethical possibility as well. My responses to bread are fundamental to my way in the world with and among others. In this way, the actual bread makes questions and demands, obligations.

Let the eating of bread stand for the reading of the scripture. To bind oneself to the text is a movement both of renewed imagination and renewed ethical life. The body of the text is not only a sign for meaning, but also a sign of the bodies, the lives of others. It is a claim, a witness to the "at-stake-ness" of interpretation. The Other is not an idea any more than the Word of God is an idea. Whatever I may think or imagine about the Other, the actual life of the Other (the face of the Other as Levinas says) claims my response and judges my response. The written word is a sign of speech itself in all of its promise, deception, power, fragility, truthfulness, and limitation. The written word is a sign of the community of speech and what it costs us to speak and listen, to hear and respond. The words on the page, their physical presence on the page, is a witness that calls to the reader to return again and again to the life of speech and its freedom and obligation. Surely, this too is what it means to interpret a text by loving the neighbor, the actual neighbor.

> Bless thou the truth, dear Lord, to me, to me,
> As thou didst bless the bread by Galilee;
> Then shall all bondage cease, all fetters fall,
> And I shall find my peace, my all in all.
>
> — Mary Lathbury

The holiness of scripture for an interpreter will often be expressed through the term "revelation." The question of revelation may be seen to share the same structure as the question of holiness. They are parallel terms in different regions. In a kind of onto-theological frame, one could say that revelation is to epistemology as holiness is to ontology. Revelation stands in relation to knowledge as holiness does to being. The parallel term in the (mediating) realm of language would be truth. Revelation is the question of holiness and "truth" worked out in terms of texts and experience.

As a contemporary theological question it is indeed problematic. Some insist it is so thoroughly premodern a concept that it cannot be retrieved. Others argue that it can be intelligible and meaningful (and may well be crucial) within the language and symbol systems of Judeo-Christian faith, if not to those outside. Still others say it is universally valid and binding, intelligible or not, believed or not.[11]

The term "revelation" itself suggests disclosure, unveiling, manifestation, the showing of something. God warns and instructs Noah. Abraham is given a promise. Jacob receives a dream. God calls to Moses from a burning bush, leads Israel out with a mighty hand and an outstretched arm, gives the law at Sinai, meets Moses face to face in the tent of meeting. Prophets receive visions and speak a word from God. Gentile rulers become the instruments of liberation. Angels announce glad tidings. Miracles and healings are performed. The realm of God is depicted in teachings and parables. The sky darkens, earthquakes shake, a curtain is torn. Death and resurrection, a meal, promises of presence. Mighty deeds, signs and wonders, visions and dreams. Appearances. Interpretation. The multiple depictions of this in the Bible themselves suggest a process of *revealing* more than so fixed a concept as *revelation*.

We may speak commonly of revelation as an event or history, as a body of knowledge or doctrine (textual or oral), as an experience or awareness.[12] In traditional theological usage it has typically been founded on the dynamic of God granting knowledge. Such knowledge is either of a kind that would otherwise be unknowable, or of a degree that so clarifies what is known (whether by reason, experience, or intuition) that it becomes an organizing paradigm for reality. The question was traditionally structured with the same dynamics as the question of nature and grace, with reason and experience corresponding to the former, and revelation to the latter. The relations between the two were frequently complex and intertwining. Thus Paul could speak of the law being known by the gentiles. Augustine could say that wherever the truth was, it is God's. Calvin could depict the scriptures as eyeglasses that allowed one to see clearly, and Schleiermacher could appeal to a universal human sense of absolute dependence as foundation of an understanding of revelation. Following Kant, however, the difference between the two poles tends to become hardened, and the distance between fixed as a chasm. An idea of revelation is then set in opposition to an idea of reason and experience, and both are set up as independent regions with nothing to say to one another. Revelation becomes "authoritarian and opaque" (Ricoeur) while reason and experience suppose they are autonomous and transparent.[13]

When the question of revelation is raised in relation to the scriptures, its meaning is usually tied to the issues of truth and authority. What kind of truth and authority do the scriptures have? Where do they it come from? How do they work in the life of the community? What do they imply for interpretation? Often, however, the question is detached from the Bible itself and the multiple ways in which its various forms of writing testify. In place of the dynamic and plural possibilities of the Bible, one form of revelation and authority is presented. Ironically, it happens that out of a desire to secure the status of the scriptures, the scriptures themselves — what they say and how they say it — are set aside.

Rather than asking what sort of revelation the Bible is as a whole, let us ask instead how within the Bible the writings themselves testify to what revelation might be. Paul Ricoeur proposes that this is precisely what the different kinds of writing do. They are the "originary expressions" or confessions of faith, prior to codification or dogmatization. They present and preserve the traces in language of how God was believed to be known. As witness, they reveal revelation, we might say, as it is depicted from one side.

Ways of knowing

> The naming of God, in the originary expressions of faith, is not simple but multiple. It is not a single tone, but polyphonic. The originary expressions of faith are complex forms of discourse as diverse as narratives, prophecies, laws, proverbs, prayers, hymns, liturgical formulas, and wisdom writings. As a whole these forms of discourse name God. But they do so in various ways.[14]

The idea of revelation itself is commonly wed to one such form of witness, the prophetic oracle.[15] The particular witness of that one form is then expanded into a general idea of revelation, silencing the other possibilities that the scriptures themselves propose. If we could summarize the form of the oracle by the introductory announcement "Thus says Yahweh . . . ," this becomes the model for what revelation means. Revelation figured in this way means a double speaking. There is a voice behind the voice of the prophet, the voice of God. The words of the prophet are identified as the Word of Yahweh. The words are revealed by God to the prophet, and by the prophet to the people. This model — we could call it a divine authorship model — then takes priority and becomes the basic paradigm of what it means to speak of revelation (whether it is accepted or rejected). This is, indeed, a vitally important dynamic within scripture with which an interpreter must come to terms, but it is not the *only* dynamic, and to understand what revelation might signify only through this one mode imposes a most unbiblical singularity upon the scriptural witness.

Affirming multiple possibilities, of course, does not by itself take away the difficulty of the idea of revelation. It may indeed *multiply* the difficulty, because revelation would not mean only one thing, but many things. One could argue, however, that this restores the *proper* difficulty of revelation by restoring its ultimate dynamism and mystery. The understanding of divine accommodation affirmed that God reveals Godself to humankind according to our capacities and limitations. We know only as much of God as the human mind, heart, and body can perceive. We see humanly, because that is the only way we *can* see. Were we angels that would be a different matter. Human beings, therefore, cannot attain to superhuman knowledge. The distinction between general revelation and special revelation becomes one of degree or emphasis. Whatever knowledge we have will have to be within the realm of sense, reason, experience, intuition, and imagination, and to speak as if we had some other kind of knowledge would be false. Revelation then is not some small and special kind of knowledge, but embraces all of our ways of knowing. It is human knowledge as such — and still remains incomplete, and distinctly human. What we know as the truth of God is not an alien truth, but a human truth. The question then becomes one of "canon" and "canon within the canon." Within what we know where do we find trustworthy centers around which to gather?

The Bible presents multiple ways of knowing, multiple dimensions of knowing, multiple expressions of knowing. It configures different relationships of knowing, contexts of knowing, confessions of knowing. These all invite different kinds of participation. They propose, communicate, and promise different kinds of authority. Because of this rich polyphony of possibilities, revelation becomes a *question* posed to the interpreter, not an *answer* about the text. As ways of knowing, relationship, and response, these different genres require and invite different dimensions of one's spiritual praxis. One engages what they know, how they know it, and the implications of that way of knowing for one's response. This includes, of course, the response of one's own speaking, including (but by no means limited to) preaching. Interpretation is then the *confession* made in response by one who *bears witness*.

To unfold some central dynamics of this, let us consider several of the most important genres of the scripture's own witness: narrative, law or torah, prophecy, parable, wisdom, and psalmody.

A storied world

One could argue that within the Bible all the other forms take on their distinctive voice and authority in the response to narrative.[16] That is, they presuppose a larger narrative frame in which they live and move and have their being. Exactly what that frame is, of course, is disputed within the Bible itself, as various kinds of criticism have shown over the last century or so. Sometimes, as we can see in clashes between prophets such as Jeremiah and Hananiah, that dispute is the very subject matter of the scriptures themselves. Sometimes, as with the stranger on the road to Emmaus, the goal of understanding the scriptures at all is to get the story right.

Biblical narrative is not *one* thing, with only one set of motives or criteria. Adele Berlin observes that in the Hebrew Bible itself there is not a term for narrative as such.[17] There are parables, songs, oracles — different forms that tell or include stories — and there are vast numbers of stories of different kinds, yet the word "story" itself does not appear (*midrash* is rendered as story sometimes in English, but it has its own distinctive meaning). Not only are there very different kinds of stories, the stories can have very different kinds of interest religiously, politically, historically, or even artistically. With such an array of differing motives and styles, generalization is difficult, indeed. Nevertheless, both Testaments place an extended "history-like" telling at the core and keep returning to that telling to retell, reflect, revise, reverse, and ultimately to reveal God's nature, action, intention, and promise for the world.

In this sense, narrative is a form of confession (as all the biblical forms may be understood to be). As a confession, biblical narrative points first of all to founding events or history (or at least history-like chronicles) as the place of God's self-disclosure. It is not first of all God's communication of knowledge, but God's action that such stories depict. Narrative confesses by its very form God's trace in the event-full life of the world. The disclosure takes place in the history itself, not in the words about the history. The interpreter is directed to look beyond the words themselves, to what they recount. The very style of biblical narrative, with its seemingly narrator-less omniscient point of view, emphasizes this.[18] As testimony, it disguises its quality as testimony by attempting a kind of transparency. There are, of course, many narrative subvariations that have distinctive features, but it is first of all by means of an extended and enormously complex story that the faith of Israel and the church is fundamentally witnessed.

The story that is presented, in its own terms, depicts a "world." That is, it presents a model of reality in which thinking, acting, meaning, and believing are possible.[19] It proposes a great horizon within which the community can understand and tell its own story, and the stories that make up that story. The world is proposed to our imagination, an alternative world that apart from its narration would be by no means self-evident.[20] Indeed, the claim of the story is often that the testimony of the narration is necessary to grasp the story at all. The bare events themselves seem to tell a different story entirely, even the very opposite story. To follow the entwining of the different strands, sometimes hidden, sometimes visible, to trace them as they form new patterns with one another, is to understand more and more the shape and dynamics of the world the narration presents.

The biblical story sheds its light forward, however, not backward. That is, it does not show us what happened "behind the text" but rather, it projects this world "in front of" the text. It does not give us the events themselves; it gives us the proposed world these events make. When 1 and 2 Kings tell the story of the Hebrew monarchies, for example, the particular and peculiar events that make up that story are told in service of an overarching vision of a world in which God and the Hebrews encounter one another through political, moral, and religious life. The telling of "how things were" is for the sake of telling "how things are" in a world that works that way. That world may be entered imaginatively, and analytically. We can plot out its patterns and values. We may discern what possibilities for thinking, acting, and believing it proposes. We can consider these possibilities ethically, theologically, existentially, and philosophically. We can reject or accept some or all of these possibilities, and come to understand ourselves and our own world in light of what the world of the text proposes. That is, we can interpret. But that narrated world remains different from all our interpretation, open to yet other possibilities, so that interpretation must return again and again, because no interpretation is adequate to the complexity of what the story has and can yet disclose.

As a way of knowing, then, narrative both invites and confronts. It invites imagination to see a world, to identify with and within that world, and to discern the possibilities it presents for understanding, believing, and being. The narrative elements of setting, plot, character, and the narration itself include the interpreter in the work of place naming, acting, forming personhood, and telling it into story. To participate as an interpreter is to *enter into* the construction of the story, not simply receive it. That is, it models a kind of responsibility. It confronts the world or worlds within my own imagination and calls them to account. It undercuts the world that seems so self-evident to me by disclosing it as a told world, too, which could be told differently. It questions how

I have named my place, plotted out my life, formed a character, and told it all into a story.

Now any imaginative construction can do this (not simply narrative, or simply biblical narrative), but biblical narrative's particular (but not exclusive) invitation and confrontation challenge the reader to a *historical* act of imagination and response. It confesses a world that is actual, and in which one can (indeed, must) act.

A historical act of imagination, as I mean it (as distinct from a mythological or mystical one), is one that seeks to respond by taking responsibility.[21] Because history cannot be encompassed in our knowledge, thereby excusing us from ourselves by insisting "it's just the way things are," one must take responsibility. That is, I must confess my own choices and actions and reasons as my own, a life and history I have made in the face of a history and situation that cannot be objectively decided. To step beyond a fiction of absolute knowledge and certainty requires an act of faith in which I give myself to responsibility. As a way of knowing, narrative presents the interpreter with the spiritual task of historical responsibility: a practice of the imagination, naming and placing, choosing, personhood, and telling into story.

Knowing by doing

> Moses convened all Israel, and said to them: Hear, O Israel, the statutes and ordinances that I am addressing to you today; you shall learn them and observe them diligently.
>
> —Deuteronomy 5:1

The knowing of law and commandment is different from the knowing of an oracle or a narrative. When *Torah* is understood as teaching or way, legal or prescriptive discourse becomes a way of knowing by doing. To hear is to do, to do is to know. If one hears but does not do, one may know *about* the teaching, but one does not know the teaching itself. The teaching is first to be heard, then recognized and embodied, and then pondered, meditated upon.

The scene depicted in Deuteronomy 5–6 expresses this is in a marvelously compressed way. Moses assembles all of Israel and puts before them the commandments of God who had spoken with them face to face at the mountain, out of the fire (Deut. 5:4) — face to face, yet with Moses interposed nonetheless. The people themselves had asked for Moses to go near to God on their behalf. They knew that someone, even they, could hear the voice of God and live, yet such knowledge was too terrifying. Instead, they say, let Moses go, hear, and repeat what God says, that they may listen and do (5:22–27). Let there be a way to *live* before God that the community can survive. So Moses did as the people asked, and did as God charged him in turn. So he spoke, saying,

> Hear, O Israel: the Lord is our God, the Lord alone. You shall love the Lord your God with all your heart and with all your soul, and with all your might. Keep these words that I am commanding you today in your heart. Recite them to your children and talk about them when you are at home and when you are away, when you lie down and when you rise. Bind them as a sign upon your hand, fix them as an emblem on your forehead, and write them on the doorposts of your house and on your gates. (Deut. 6:4–9)

Performing the commandments of God is the embodiment of the love of God that claims heart, soul, and strength. It claims inside and outside, the house and the road, the day and the night, rest and work, going out and coming in. It is performed as a sign and worn as a sign. It is a sign of the covenant between Israel and the God who has set them free and prepared a land for them. The law testifies God to Israel, and by keeping the law, Israel testifies God to themselves, and before the nations. The keeping of the commandments is the actual form of memory and hope. Where is the memory of God's deeds? Where is the hope and trust in God's sworn promise? In the keeping of the commandments. Therefore, when the children ask what the law means, it becomes the time to bind the life of the community to the story once again. Keeping the commandments is how one is part of this community of memory and hope.

When Jesus says, "Whoever does the will of God is my brother, sister, and mother" (Mark 3:35), he is echoing this founding Torah truth: the knowing is in the doing, and in the doing is the relationship to God and the witnesses of God. Jesus' words in Matthew press even farther. Not only does one know the will of God by doing the will of God, it is in doing the will of God that one is known. To those who have spoken the right words and even lifted up his name, if they have not done the will of God, he says, "I will declare to them, 'I never knew you'" (Matt. 7:23).

The way of knowing that the commandments bring, then, is neither the same as the way of knowing by story, nor can it be separated from the story. The story without the keeping of the commandment testifies only to forgetfulness. Its very recitation in the absence of keeping the teaching is a judgment upon the teller. The recitation is forgetfulness disguised as remembrance, and all the more forgetful because it forgets that it has forgotten. The true sign of remembrance is the love of God with heart, soul, and might, the keeping of the law. An oracle of Jeremiah promises that this way of knowing and doing will finally become Israel's very nature. The law will no longer need to be bound to one's body or taught to others, because God says, "I will put my law within them, and write it on their hearts; and I will be their God, and they shall be my people. No longer shall they teach one another, or say to each other, 'Know the Lord,' for they shall all know me, from the least of them to the greatest" (Jer. 31:33–34). Israel itself becomes the inscription of the teaching. In the same way Paul wrote to the Corinthians, "You yourselves are our letter, written on your hearts, to be known and read by all; and you show that you are a letter of Christ prepared by us, written not with ink but with the Spirit of the living God, not on tablets of stone but on tablets of human hearts" (2 Cor. 3:2–3). The ultimate aim of the law, therefore, is to be transformed into the actual life of the community, which Paul insists can happen even apart from the law. When the gentile doers of the law "who do not possess the law, do instinctively what the law requires, these, though not having the law, are a law to themselves. They show that what the law requires is written on their hearts, to which their own conscience also bears witness" (Rom. 2:14–15).

As a way of knowing, then, action and narration are bound together. As spiritual practice it is, indeed, a praxis. The ordinary ways of person and community are claimed as meaningful expressions of memory and relationship with God, and therefore are to be reflected upon, interrogated, understood, and corrected. To enter into an interpretive relationship with Torah faithfulness means those acts that are undertaken and narrated as an expression of relationship with God.

The Teaching is bound to the Teacher. The Teacher is met in the story. The story is enacted in discipleship. Discipleship is life in relationship: we know by following. If you want to know Jesus, you must go with Jesus down the road (John 12:26).

Call, re-calling, re-membering, standing in the place of truth

> Then I heard the voice of the Lord saying, "Whom shall I send, and who will go for us?" And I said, "Here am I; send me."
> —Isaiah 6:8

We considered the prophetic oracle in its formal description as a speech-act, with its configuration of a voice behind a voice behind a text. But the prophetic proclamations point to other dimensions of the ways of knowing called revelation. While prophets may be found in the context of a primarily cultic disclosure, ecstatic, overwhelmed, possessed ("Is Saul among the prophets?"), the depiction of biblical prophets is decisively of a different character. Vital dimensions of this character could be summarized by the themes of *call, re-calling and re-membering,* and *standing in the place of the truth.* There is a kind of continuity from one theme to another, or perhaps a mutual echoing of one by another.

Prophetic call stories may be seen as having similar structures, and may be thought of as a kind of form themselves.[22] Whether it is Moses and the burning bush, the angel appearing to Gideon, Isaiah in the temple, the bare coming of the Word of the Lord to Jeremiah, or Ezekiel's vision of the scroll of lamentation, mourning, and woe offered to him to eat, they begin with a confrontation. In this confrontation what becomes immediately clear is that to be Moses or Isaiah or the others now means to be summoned specifically as the person each one is. God names God's own identity as caller and sender ("I am . . . I send you"), and thereby summons the prophet to a new vocation, a new self-hood. This self-hood is constituted by a call and a commission. The call singles out the prophet, makes the prophet an exception; the commission binds the prophet to the community. "If just one is called, a whole people is intended."[23]

To be singled out, then, is to be singled out *from* and *for.* A prophet is singled out from the past, which may be prologue but is not qualification. If Moses is the most extended example, his own argument (which God does not dispute) is that he is unqualified (Isaiah and Jeremiah say the same). Even growing up in Pharaoh's court as a prince of Egypt neither equips nor prevents him from being a prophet. Neither qualification nor disqualification matter. They are irrelevant because God will finally be the one who speaks. In one sense, the prophet is singled out from being Moses so that he can become Moses. The identity of Moses lies in the future. He is singled out *for* the future.

The prophet is also singled out from the community, for the community. The prophet must call the community to itself, to its true history and identity, for the sake of its true future and vocation. For the sake of the community, then, the prophet is placed over against the community. The prophet must emerge from the community in order to face the community, and indeed, be faced by the community. The *face* of the prophet can be terrifying, because it reflects the divine summons and command. For that very reason, the prophet and community must stand face to face. It is not, after all, only the community that does not want to see the face of the prophet; prophets, too, can dread the face of the community. This is not only because the prophet finds the ways of the community intolerable, but because it is the face of the people God loves, and seeks to give mercy. Jonah would be only too happy to turn his back, but God sends him face first. The prophetic word is ultimately one of justice *and* mercy. Neither is abstract; both must be enacted before the face of the other. Prophetic truth is bound to this identity before the face of God and the community God loves.

This leads to the second theme of re-calling and re-membering. Prophetic truth is bound to the ways of knowing that Story and Teaching embody first. The call of the prophet to the community is to re-call the story by renewing their keeping of the teaching, thereby re-membering the relationship that has been forgotten and betrayed. "I have been the Lord your God ever since the land of Egypt.... It was I who fed you in the wilderness.... Return, O Israel, to the Lord your God" (Hos. 13:4–5; 14:1).

The judgment of God is rooted in relationship and mutuality, and that relationship and mutuality are rooted in a shared story. In Isaiah, the prophet sings the bitter "Song of the Vineyard" depicting the destruction that has already befallen the people because of betrayal. Lands are swallowed up, bloodshed overtakes justice, the innocent are deprived of their rights, the rule of money replaces the rule of righteousness. The very life of the community is already testimony and judgment both (Isa. 5).

Through Amos God asks, "Did you bring to me sacrifices and offerings the forty years in the wilderness, O house of Israel?" Pseudo-memory substitutes festivals and assemblies, sacrifices and offerings for justice and righteousness (Amos 5:21–25). Mere recollection takes the place of re-calling, that is, of telling the story in such a way that the call to be a holy people is heard and taken up again into the living and testimony of the teaching. The prophet re-calls the community to the knowing characteristic of prophetic truth: "For I desire steadfast love and not sacrifice, the knowledge of God rather than burnt offerings" (Hos. 6:6). Note the parallelism: steadfast love *is* the knowledge of God. And steadfast love, whatever its inward reality might be, has the outward shape of justice and righteousness. It is possible, of course, that even the teaching can become distorted and turned into its opposite. If the purpose of the teaching is to give outward expression of steadfast love, what happens when teaching is kept but without the relationship? Then the teaching, too, becomes a substitute for justice and righteousness, another kind of forgetting. "You tithe mint, dill, and cummin, and have neglected the weightier matters of the law: justice and mercy and faith" (Matt. 23:23).

This second theme of prophetic truth, then, takes its force not only from the dynamic of God's speaking to and through the prophet, but also from the relationship of the prophetic proclamation to what we could call the mnemonic performance of justice and righteousness of the community. The prophet's call is to minister to the call of the community by re-membering what has been separated, the story from liturgy from the life. In this sense it is a priestly kind of ministry, a liturgical kind of ministry. When the liturgy of the community has become turned inward on itself, when it no longer is performed into the enacted teaching, the prophet's role is to lead the liturgy against the liturgy. The prophet is a priest for the community that has forgotten its calling.

The third theme of a prophetic knowing is *standing in the place of the truth*. Prophetic knowing is personal.[24] The identity of the prophet is so joined to the truth proclaimed that they share the same fate. The prophet's body is bound to the prophet's word. The prophet not only is a bearer of signs, but is a sign. To receive the prophet's word is to receive the prophet; to receive the prophet is to receive the one who sends the prophet. Whoever receives a prophet *as* (that is, because one is) a prophet shares in the future of the prophet as well (Matt. 10:41). The community has separated memory from teaching and life and supposes that these can be separated and the community still live. In a most immediate way, the prophet demonstrates what it means to join memory, teaching, and life. Oddly enough, the prophet embodies a kind of wholeness. I say oddly, because it is certainly not the kind of psychic wholeness so often depicted in models of mental equilibrium or spiritual health. But a prophetic wholeness discloses the real fragmentation of the community by its sheer tension with the pseudo-wholeness of forgetfulness (which becomes whole by turning inward upon itself). As a way of knowing, then, prophecy joins person, action, and speech in such a way that they cannot be separated. They may be rejected or accepted, but not separated. Surely the most poignant expression of this is in Jeremiah's lament,

> For the word of the Lord has become for me
> a reproach and derision all day long.
> If I say, "I will not mention [God]
> or speak any more in [God's] name,"
> then within me there is something like a burning fire,
> shut up in my bones;
> I am weary with holding it in,
> and I cannot. (Jer. 20:8–9)

The reader who turns to the words of the prophets, then, is presented with more than a content, whether that of fore-telling or forth-telling. Prophetic disclosure, or revelation if you will, confronts the reader with a way of knowing that can only be followed down the same path of call, re-calling and re-membering, and standing in the place of the truth. The proclamation of the prophets calls the community as a community among the communities to the same stance as the prophet has taken with them. It is the community itself that is called to be prophetic, and the individual prophet is required only where the community has forsaken its calling. Insofar as the prophet has a word from the Lord, the aim of that word is to be given to the hearers in such a way that they too can prophesy in the same integrity. The prophet who faithfully shares the given word has nothing more than the community to which the word is given: no secret knowledge, no special qualification the community lacks. It is the Word that makes a prophet, and only by sharing what has been given does one fulfill the vocation. The prophet who holds back what God has given is guilty of the blood of the community.

"Consider your own call, brothers and sisters..." (1 Cor. 1:26). Consider your own call, preacher. What is the word that re-calls you to it, re-members you to it, and in which you stand and bear witness for the community to see?

Speaking in parables

> A sower went out to sow his seed...
> —Luke 8:5

"Jesus told the crowds all these things in parables; without a parable he told them nothing" (Matt. 13:14). Speaking in parables is characteristic of Jesus' public ministry as it is depicted in the synoptic Gospels. It might seem that this would then be some kind of key to understanding who Jesus was and what he said; instead his parables have proven to be more of a mirror for those who interpret them. This happens already in the gospel stories.

Time and again by a saying, a story, or a riddle, Jesus' questioners find that their question has turned back upon them. They seek to expose Jesus, only to find themselves exposed.

It has happened when commentators in every age of the church have elucidated the parables, finding in them the meanings they prize already. Take the parable of the sower and the seed, for instance. The multiplying yield of grain thirty-, sixty-, and a hundredfold becomes in the hands of Jerome the merit of married persons, the widowed and continent, and virgins. Elsewhere the married drop out from the lowest rung so that the martyrs may be placed on the highest. Gregory the Great offered faith in the Trinity, good works, and the life of contemplation of eternity. To Christian of Stablo, the fact that the numbers are all multiples of ten corresponded to the Trinity (30), the six days of creation (60), and the perfect number (10 x 10).[25]

Although the results are very different, something similar happens also with present-day inquirers. Interpreters take up the meaning and method of parables, only to find that they reveal more about the meanings and methods of the interpreters than of Jesus. What are parables? Simple object lessons, vivid teaching stories drawn from everyday life, spiritual allegories, paradoxical sayings, inside codes, insoluble riddles, perception-altering existential apocalypses, revolutionary political-economic critiques, poetical word-tricks — commentators have found all these and more as the key to Jesus' parables.[26] And there is truth enough in any one of these views to account for some, not enough truth in all of them together to account for all.

If parables were indeed characteristic of Jesus' public ministry, then, as William Herzog points out, they must have something awfully important to do with why he was executed.[27] Whatever they were about, and however listeners responded to them, it threatened political, religious, and economic interests enough to get Jesus killed. It is not simply a matter of what the parables are about, I believe. That would tend to make them into husks of meaning that can be discarded when one has gotten the point.[28] There is something about how parables actually work, or more accurately, how readers and listeners work with parables, that also matters. John Dominic Crossan made the distinction among myth, apologue, action, satire, and parable. Myth could be said to found and establish a world. Apologue maintains and justifies a world. Action explores and describes a world. Satire questions a world. Parables *subvert* a world.[29] "The Jesus parables are not myth; they are anti-myth."[30] Into a myth of order they introduce disorder; in a dream of a put-together world, they are world-shattering. And if they are indeed world-shattering, it is because of how they lead readers and listeners to see, imagine, and think about the way things are and the way they might be. To subversive content is joined a subversive process, which leads to a subversive way of being in the world.

This is the sense in which parable is a way of knowing, a kind of revelation. As revelation it is different from narrative, oracle, or law, because it directs one toward a different point of disclosure. The parable does not say, "In the eighteenth year of...." The parable does not say, "Set apart a tithe of all the yield of your seed." The parable does not say, "Thus says the Lord." The parable says, The reign of God is like... a woman with leaven, a merchant searching for fine pearls. The parable says, an owner had a vineyard. A traveler went down from Jerusalem to Jericho. In a city there was a judge. A shepherd had a hundred sheep.

Frustrated with my refusal (or inability) to say what the meaning of a particular parable was, a person once listened very politely to my explanation of how parables do what they do. He sat silently shaking his head and then finally said, "If parables don't give answers, maybe that's because they're the tests, to see what you really know." I believe he was right. Whatever the parable gives, it is not given hand to hand. In fact, rather than giving a single correct meaning (making the parable itself redundant), it requires the listener to *make* meaning. Out of what? Out of the distance and difference between what the parable says and the place it is heard. "Parable is not primarily didactic, it is primarily hermeneutic."[31] The parable requires you to re-examine what you already know, and the more you must re-examine the stronger the parable. Parable forces one out into what Ricoeur called the "itineraries of meaning" that move through the Bible, those itineraries that twist and turn, entwine, reverse, sometimes collide as the trace through the paths of the biblical world.[32] Parables provoke and disclose the intertextuality at work, especially the tears and gaps that one was not even aware of. In this sense, the death of Jesus is a parable — for Christians the parable of parables — as the stranger on the road in Luke's Gospel told it when he interpreted all of Moses and the prophets (Luke 24:25–27). For the reader it is all the more a parable, because while the disciples may hear the teaching, the reader does not.[33] The stranger on the road asks the question, but it is the reader who must answer it, and the only way to answer is to go back to all of Moses and the prophets. Take any given parable and ask yourself how many different questions it provokes. Ask yourself where you must begin to begin to answer them, and then where next, and where next and where next. And even there you must ask again: where next? This is parabolic knowing.

The itineraries of meaning, however, are not restricted to the world of the Bible, as Herzog insisted, because that's not why Jesus was executed. To limit itineraries of meaning to the Bible would be an exceedingly non-parabolic thing to do. If the parable of the workers in the vineyard does not go by way of the unemployment office and the guy trying to wash your windshield at the stoplight, it has become something else. The parable in particular works in the gaps: between text and text, between text and life, between life and life. Thus the "hearing and grasping of a parable is a process leading a hearer through a series of stages."[34] What is disclosed is disclosed *there*, in the places the parable leads. The question is whether the interpreter will follow the parable or not.

As a way of knowing, then, parable is paradoxically both self-effacing and indispensable. It is self-effacing insofar as it is always leading out elsewhere, into narratives, law, prophecy, wisdom, lament, out into the hedgerows and byways of experience to include more and more. It is indispensable insofar as it never disappears and dissolves into the places it leads, but angles off again like a rolling coin and forces you to follow to its new destination. The parable is no respecter of texts or interpreters. Catch it, put it in your pocket, and it either finds the hole or makes one. This, too, is how the Bible does the work of revelation.

To the disciples Jesus says, "To you has been given the mystery of the reign of God, but for those outside, everything comes in parables" (Mark 4:11). It is a hard saying, and gets harder as his words continue. He seems to say that parables are for the *purpose* of keeping the outsiders to God's reign outside. It is tempting to try to soften the implications of Jesus' words, as interpreters have often done, particularly in the face of a meaning that is difficult or even scandalous, one that doesn't fit with the understanding of Jesus that I like best. But in Mark's Gospel, even those who have been given the mystery of the reign of God still don't get the parable of the seed and the soils, so if getting it means you are an insider, they are outsiders, too; so who is left? It appears that even being given the mystery doesn't give you the key. The mystery gives you the mystery, not the solution. The secret gives you the secret *as* a secret, and no other way. The mystery is not hidden, so it is all the more mystery. Ultimately, it is Jesus himself, and to follow where the parables lead is the same as following Jesus. To follow Jesus is to enter into his own parable.

> O it's Jesus in the desert with the wild beasts and the pain,
> And it's Jesus with the devil urging trade it all for gain.
> O it's finding and it's losing, and it's gaining and it's loss,

And it's counting down the benefits and counting up the
    costs.
O it's Jesus with the prostitute and Jesus with the thief,
And Jesus with the lepers and the mourners and the grief.
O it's preaching on the mountain, and teaching on the plain,
And praying in the garden where the sweat falls down like
    rain.
O it's Jesus at Golgotha, and Jesus at the end,
And Jesus wrapped in linen by the kindness of a friend.
O it's waiting through the awful day, and waiting through
    the night,
And it's angels with the women at the rising of the light.
And it's Jesus standing upright in the flowering of the tomb,
And it's Jesus at the table, and Jesus in the room.

Wisdom

Pride goes before destruction,
and a haughty spirit before a fall.
It is better to be of a lowly spirit among the poor
than to divide the spoil with the proud.

—Proverbs 16:18–19

Within the range of the Bible is included a kind of writing that would seem to be the precise opposite of the dynamic of revelation the prophetic oracle presents. If prophecy points to the voice of a hidden speaker disclosing what can be known no other way, if prophecy seeks a "transaudiency" like the translucency that lets light pass through, wisdom makes no such claim. Rather than "Thus says Yahweh . . . " wisdom evokes the voice of the sage, the teacher, the ruler, the cynic, the observer, the innocent sufferer. Wisdom considers the actual life of the world that is spread out plain for all to see. It seeks to trace the immanent design, to *see* how things are, to know, to comment upon, to find consolation or encouragement within the terms of existence.

Wisdom is concerned with what becomes of righteousness, and the outcome of virtue; it is also concerned, therefore, with suffering and injustice, and the outcome of evil. Often what one finds, then, is instruction in how to live righteously. It is not the instruction of law; it presupposes no special covenant, except whatever covenant it is that makes some kind of order in the world. Wisdom speaks of a conception of the world as such, and the person as such, and what happens when the two meet: cosmos, ethos, pathos.[35] It presents the value of truth, honesty, integrity, humility, honoring God, judiciousness in speech, friendship, marriage, and sexuality. It does not so much make a promise as attempt to persuade that such attitude and action lead to a good life, contentment, honor, offspring, and length of years. Even the experiences that would seem to make such assurance manifestly false are themselves undercut by a deeper design that will yet come to light.

Sometimes it reflects the confidence of a settled world, at peace with how things happen. Sometimes it reflects a bright world gone into twilight, night approaching, in which all bets are off. The sun will not show anything new, nor will the darkness hide anything old. Here, indeed, the seam works loose. The experience of contradiction, the truth of experience pulling just the other way threatens to tear the garment apart: evil, chance, and death against goodness, order, and life. Look to the way things are done on earth, how God seems to be working in the lives of the righteous, and you will find no answer. "Whether it is love or hate one does not know. Everything that confronts them is vanity, since the same fate comes to all, to the righteous and the wicked, to the good and the evil..." (Eccles. 9:1–2).

What may be most astonishing about the wisdom literature included in the Bible is how fully the conflict is allowed out in the open, and how little harmony is imposed — or at least how fully the discouragement and world-weariness are given their say. Even the counsel of equivocation is brought forward and permitted to stand.

> In my vain life I have seen everything: there are righteous people who perish in their righteousness, and there are wicked people who prolong their life in their evil-doing. Do not be too righteous, and do not act too wise: why should you destroy yourself? Do not be too wicked, and do not be a fool; why should you die before your time? It is good that you should take hold of the one, without letting go of the other for the one who fears God shall succeed with both.
>
> (Eccles. 7:15–18)

So wisdom can mean moderation even in righteousness and wickedness. A little wickedness, a little foolishness, for neither one will protect you. Better to play both ends; somehow, even this can be done, for one who fears God will still succeed with righteousness in one hand, wickedness in the other. What may be particularly shocking is that this counsel seems more true to experience than assurances of how things are *supposed* to go for the righteous and the evil-doer. If the measure is some kind of success — getting things done, getting through, or just plain surviving — then this counsel sounds empirically true. In any case, it is more realistic about the actual ability of conflicted people in a conflicted world; it offers some consolation to those who do not always choose the good, and encourages them to keep trying. As for the evil, even they may find reason enough to restrain their evil-doing, if for no other reason than to save their own necks, so the world gains a little peace in return. The passage may even be seen to suggest a sort of teleological suspension of the ethical: fearing God seems to make both righteousness and unrighteousness into a different possibility. Perhaps it is no different than the parable of the unjust servant who makes friends by means of dishonesty. Perhaps it is no different than being wise as serpents and innocent as doves. A harmonization may be imaginable wherein righteousness is not really undermined, but it will have to be imagined, because the texts themselves do not provide one.

Wisdom, nevertheless, argues that its truth can be realized in real life. It directs the reader to such arenas as work, politics, relationships, and interior life to see its truth demonstrated, if not in absolutes, then in meaningfully confirmable patterns, patterns that are not overturned by the ambiguity of life. Take as an example the way the same Ecclesiastes, which contains the cold-eyed counsel of equivocation, looks with an equally cold eye upon how the love of money works upon the shape of a person's character and the outcomes of a life. Qoheleth observes that the lovers of money will not be satisfied with money, but will only want more. The more they have, the more will be consumed by those who gather around the riches. The riches themselves lead to disastrous ventures that leave one destitute and embittered, family broken, vexed, sick, and resentful. Desire takes away what is actually in your hand and leads you out into a wandering that never reaches an end, as empty as chasing the wind. Instead, the teacher counsels, let one accept what comes as a gift of God, enjoy the work and the rest both. Rather than brooding over what one does not have, let the gift of God keep your heart in joy (Eccles. 5:10–6:9).

Jesus' parable of the rich fool is a beautiful example of this kind of wisdom (Luke 12:16–20). The rich man puts up more storehouses to hold all the abundance that has come to him. The goods seem to represent the assurance of the future. The question of the future is taken away and is figured as an extension of the power of his wealth. To gaze upon his wealth is to see his future. But God says to him, "You fool! This very night...." Now let us pause for a moment here, because the usual translations say something like "your soul [or life] is being demanded of you" (NRSV). Yet the verb in the Greek text is not passive, and not in the second person; it is active, and in the third person. That is, the text would read, "This very night *they demand* your life of you." Who are *they,* but the storehouses and goods? This gives a much more eerie reading to the final verse, "And the things you have prepared, whose will they be?" The goods have taken the fool's life, and now they may indeed go on to take the life of another fool.

Casting its shadow over the search for wisdom is the fact of suffering and death. At its most serious, it is because of this dimension of experience that the seeker asks for wisdom. In the face of *this* how is one to view the world and God? In the face of *this* how is one to live? "Wisdom does not teach us how to avoid suffering, or how magically to deny it, or how to dissimulate under an illusion. It places suffering into a meaningful context by producing the active quality of suffering."[36] That is, suffering is transformed from something simply to be borne into something to be engaged, questioned, protested. If Job is the most profound example of this in wisdom literature, then this engagement is directed even to God. Job's demand for meaning refuses to be consoled with any explanation that does not take the issue of justice with the greatest seriousness. Even the action of God is not released from confrontation. It is not for human beings to suppose that we have encompassed wisdom in such a way that it is now contained in what we can think and say. The offense of innocent suffering is so grave that it exceeds our gravest explanations and doctrines. The question must not be silenced by mere answers. It must be responded to by God. Even if the reply of God is incomprehensible, it is what the seriousness of the question of suffering requires. Meaning does not necessarily mean explanation, which may not be possible to incorporate into the speech and reason available to humankind.[37] Meaning presses beyond explanation to response. Wisdom seeks the "meaning of meaning."[38]

In this way, the search for wisdom may be seen to turn to the dimension of disclosure and relationship that characterize law and prophecy. There is a kind of wisdom that is not exhausted, perhaps not even imagined by one's observation of how things are in the world. Wisdom is ultimately figured as God's divine partner, the co-worker in whom God delights. In turn Wisdom rejoices also in the world God has made and the human race (Prov. 8:22–31). She is at work in the world, teaching and warning even as the prophets do. She can be heard, learned from, attended, followed, loved. Thus the highest goal of wisdom is the meeting of understanding and love in the ambiguous and mysterious arena of life.

"Teach us to number our days that we may get a heart of wisdom" (Ps. 90:12). Whatever wisdom is, whatever a wise heart is, it means knowing what day it is, what a day is *for,* and how to live that day.

Teach us to number our days: days of mourning and rejoicing, separating and joining, leaving and returning, silence and celebration. Teach us to number our days: the day of work and the day of rest, a day for justice, a day for mercy, a day to be alone, a day to be together, a day for family, a day for the stranger (and even the enemy). Teach us to number our days: evening and morning, one day; seedtime and harvest, a year; first breath and last breath, a lifetime. Wisdom means knowing how to live a day that no one has ever seen before, and which will never be repeated. Teach us to number *this* day.

Hymning and healing

Be merciful to me, O God, be merciful to me,
   for in you my soul takes refuge;
   in the shadow of your wings I will take refuge,
   until the destroying storms pass by.   —Ps. 57:1

In answer to the letter of a sick friend, Athanasius, archbishop of Alexandria, wrote a treatise on the interpretation of the Psalms. Known as the *Letter to Marcellinus,* his reply appears to be a kind of handbook, the earliest known example of a manual of interpretation for personal use.[39] The letter does not appear to have attracted a great deal of attention in ancient times, and modern scholars have given it small attention, as well.[40] Perhaps this is because it is pastoral and irenic rather than doctrinal and combative. Or perhaps it is because it does not do the groundbreaking work of Origen's *First Principles* and takes for granted the interpretive approaches for which Alexandria had become famous. The three-fold cord of the historical, moral, and allegorical meanings of scripture is unbroken, but the theory of interpretation is not the concern of Athanasius's writing.

He is concerned, rather, with the nature of the Psalms themselves and what we could call in contemporary terms their performance by a reader. He presents, therefore, a remarkable reflection upon the transformative possibilities of the Psalms as a *genre* through their (oral) interpretation. It is a work about interpretation in which the Psalms themselves are the actors, the subject, not the object, of what happens. It is a vision of interpretation bound to a formative and transformative discipline, turned toward the wholeness of the scriptures and the wholeness of the interpreter, focused beyond the content of interpretation (although including it) to the performance of interpretation as it flowers out from the dynamics of Psalmody. It makes, therefore, a good place to consider the ways of knowing that hymnic discourse provides, in terms already described by the fourth century CE. First, an outline of the letter.[41]

Athanasius frames his counsel as that of an old "master of the Psalter" he has consulted, and whose words he now communicates to Marcellinus. He begins with the acknowledgment that all scripture is inspired and profitable for teaching, but insists that the Psalter has particular qualities that distinguish it.

"Each sacred book supplies and announces its own promise" (par. 2). History, legislation, prophecy, admonition, and instruction all have their particular gift to give, "Yet the Book of Psalms is like a garden containing things of all these kinds, and it sets them to music, but also exhibits things of its own that it gives in song along with them" (2).

To illustrate the point the next several segments of letter present examples of the kinds of literature found within the Psalms — history, prophecy, law. He acknowledges that in the other parts of scripture the different genres also appear together, as does hymnody, because they serve the same Word by the same Spirit (9). Rather delicately, Athanasius allows that none of the writings are deficient in grace or adequacy to do what they purposed to do.

> But even so, the Book of Psalms thus has a certain grace of its own, and a distinctive exactitude of expression. For in addition to the other things in which it enjoys an affinity and fellowship with the other books, it possesses, beyond that, this marvel of its own — namely that it contains even the emotions of each soul, and it has the changes and rectification of these delineated and regulated in itself. (10)

In the other books one receives knowledge. In the Psalms "the one who hears...also comprehends and is taught in the emotions of the soul, and consequently, on the basis of that which affects [one] and by which [one] is constrained, [one] also is enabled by this book to possess the image deriving from the words" (10). That is, the Psalter's address to the emotions makes a deeper understanding possible, not simply *of* the words, but through the words to what the words depict. Note that the *hearer* is specified. The practice of reading is an oral practice, and the reader participates with the voice, not just the eyes or mind (the letter returns to this shortly). The address to the emotions makes the Psalter address each person. The instruction may be valid for *all*, but it is addressed to *each*. The dimensions of voice and emotion single out the reader as a particular person with particular identity and particular need; it *implicates* the reader.

This, in turn, yields another "astonishing thing" about the Psalter. In the other books the reader is placed in a position to overhear the words of others and to others. The reader is not Moses or Deborah; the reader is not the Canaanites or the exiles in Babylon. Yet in the Psalms, one often hears the words as being one's own. "And the one who hears is deeply moved as though he himself were speaking, and is affected by the words of the songs, as if there were his own songs" (11). The reader moves from the third person to the first person, and hears, as it were, the text's words joined to the reader's voice as if they were one. The reader takes them up as his or her own, and through them acts and speaks on the reader's own behalf before God. The Psalms give the reader confidence to bring himself or herself before God in speech. "For the Psalms comprehend the one who observes the commandment as well as the one who transgresses, and the action of each" (11).

The words of the Psalm do not simply express the reader; they disclose the reader. They are like a mirror to the singer, so that the singer might discover what is within through the help of the words that bring it to speech. "And so, on the whole, each Psalm is both spoken and composed by the Spirit so that in these same words the stirrings of our souls might be grasped, and all of them be said as concerning us, and the same issues from us as our own words, for a remembrance of the emotions in us and a chastening of our life" (12). There is, then, both communion and communication. The work of the Spirit is *experienced* in the very experience of self-recognition and re-formation.

The soul finds in the Psalms not only a mirror of itself but also the means of "therapy and correction," because this is the work of the Savior's grace. To show the exactitude of the Psalms Athanasius considers the different genres and combinations of genres represented. Not only is there narration, moral admonition, prophecy, prayer, and confession, but they also subdivide and interweave. Petition and entreaty; appeal and thanksgiving; pure petition; confession and narrative; confession, narrative, and praise; exhortation and prescription; announcement and prophecy; exhortation and praise; promise of blessedness; charging the impious and lawbreakers; invocation, and more (14). Emotion and literary form are so closely related that you could even say that the text is formed emotion. Form is the "formalization" of emotion.

Beyond this, Athanasius specifies more closely the correspondence of the Psalms in terms of the circumstances proper to their need and help: that is, the life context, the narrative situation into which they may be placed in order to give what they have to give. They combine both elements of narrative with the emotional need or state of the hearer: conflict, wounds, temptation, fear, shame, joy, confrontation with evil. Are people planning to harm you? Sing Psalm 7 and place your confidence in the God who defends you. Or "When you encounter your foes, and wisely escape them and avoid their treachery, if you want to express gratitude, summon gentle [persons], sing Psalm 33 (34) in their presence" (18).

The *musical* nature of the Psalms is critical to what they do. They are not chanted with "melodies and strains" simply for the ear's delight, but for two particular reasons. First, "because it is fitting for the Divine Scripture to praise God not in compressed speech alone, but also in the voice that is richly broadened." It is through this broadened voice that one brings all one's soul and strength to love God. Second, the harmony of the singing unites the disparate and conflicting elements of the person to make a whole. "Just as harmony unites instruments into a single sound, the parts of the soul and body may be unified in the Spirit to serve the will of God" (28). Melodic chant is a symbol of spiritual harmony, and it is God's intention that the chants be sung, so that they might bring forth harmony within and among those who sing, and between those who sing and those who hear. From fear and conflict, the soul is brought to joy and accordance with the mind of Christ (29).

Somewhat poignantly, Athanasius concludes that the Psalms need nothing but to be sung. No embellishment or correction is called for, no virtuosity required. In fact, to voice them directly lets the holy authors hear and recognize their own words and join in, and with them, the Spirit who gave them voice first. Psalmody is then a complete harmony: within and between persons, in communion with the saints, the Spirit, the mind of Christ, pleasing God (31).

What we find in this letter, then, is a surprising combination of literary criticism, hermeneutics, poetics, and pastoral care. The author offers a conception of the scriptures as a whole, not only in the interrelation of its contents, but in the interplay of its forms. He describes a poetics of transformation that works through the mutual realization of form and content, retaining the importance of both. He presents a mode of interpretation that is clearly a performance of the text, and links performance to an interior transformation of the interpreter effected through the voice. He presents a psychology of transformation, if you will, that is contextual, particular, communal, and hermeneutic.

The question of voice is of special importance here. Frederick Ruf has argued that narrative, dramatic, and lyric genres present voice in distinctive ways that reflect different dimensions of personhood.[42] Each one achieves coherence and intelligibility or comprehensiveness, but of different scope, with different characteristic qualities and different strengths of cohesion. These are seen as a result of the nature of the voice, what the voice presents, and the relationship between the two.[43] Ruf also argues that the particular voice of a genre is not only possessed by the narrator, dramatist, or lyricist, but is also *promised* to the reader. That is, the reader is offered a view-point and a speak-point to

take up. The narrative voice, for instance, is typically more distant, frequently outside or above what is narrated, cooler. The
reader is positioned in the narrator's place to see, understand,
and grasp the larger patterns and meaning. Lyric also presents
a single voice, but it is much more likely to be identified with
a particular person, from a particular viewpoint, presenting his
or her particular perspective. It strongly tends to a speech that is
more personal or intimate, even interior. It expresses response and
feeling. The dramatic voice, by contrast, usually presents plural
voices. The narrator disappears, as with narrative, but behind the
cast of characters. One is placed in the middle of the action, with
multiple characters and viewpoints expressing themselves, acting,
revealing or hiding their thoughts, with no way to know what is
behind them unless the characters present it. In the absence of a
narrative voice, the reader must supply the connecting thread or
framework that gives comprehensiveness or intelligibility.

Narrative, therefore, locates the reader as a person who sees,
knows, and understands. Drama calls forth a person who must
discern and come to understanding. Lyric calls forth a person
who empathizes, feels, and comes to self-understanding. As Ruf
says, the different voices "become paradigms of personhood, urg-
ing different natures of one's self, one's surroundings (including
others), and one's relation to those surroundings."[44] More specifically, he concludes, the voices are concerned with different senses
of intelligibility, or what we have called here different ways and
dimensions of knowing. In its own way, the *Letter to Marcellinus*
makes the same claim. The various genres of the Bible show us
different things and form us in different ways. But the lyric of the
Psalms uniquely combines the greatest scope of narrative, with
the most immediate situation, feeling, and need of the reader. A
genre of genres, we could call it, which brings the spirituality of
interpretation to the *necessity* of speech.

In the most comprehensive way, this ancient letter binds the
realization of the interpretive journey to the multiple ways of

knowing the Bible presents. It binds them not only together with each other, but also to the act of interpretation itself performed by the interpreter in the service of the healing and transformation of self and other. It binds them to the always to be discovered disclosure that happens uniquely in actual speech.

It is not only in the Psalms, of course, that the hymnic way of knowing is offered. For that matter, it isn't only in the Bible. I remember attending service once on Christmas Eve. The sanctuary was large and full; the choir moved in procession around us as the little candles of the worshipers were lit and began to illuminate the shadow-filled church. Because there were so many of us we sang hymn after hymn while the light grew. Not just the usual "Please rise as you are able," four verses, then "You may be seated," but hymn after hymn after hymn as we stood. I looked to my right, following the cross-led procession with my eyes, and noticed an older woman whose face was turned so as to catch the light. A tear had formed at the corner of her eye and slowly descended the plane of her cheek. The candle in her hand made the tear's track shine, and the drop hung briefly at the line of her jaw before falling darkly to her blouse. One tear. She sang on and on.

> Bless the Lord, O my soul, and all that is within me bless God's holy name.

Gates to the city

The Bible presents many more forms than those considered here, but these should be sufficient to demonstrate the point. Narrative, prophecy, teaching, parable, wisdom, psalmody, and the others emerge from and lead to different ways of knowing and communicating. The way of wisdom is different from the way of a parable. The way of a historical chronicle is different from that of a hymn. The way of a personal letter is different from the way of an apocalypse.

They each make their own claims of authority. They each situate the reader in certain ways. They each imply the presence or absence of the author differently. They each direct the reader's attention in a certain direction. They each invite distinctive responses. They each imply a different dimension of personhood and spiritual life.

This much may be said of any writing, indeed of any communication. A newspaper is not a phonebook, a movie is not a postcard, a song is not an essay, a kiss is not a handshake. But when we turn from talk of ways of knowing to talk of revelation the issue becomes more than a technical point for interpreters or stylists. It becomes a matter of confession, taking up a relationship in responsibility, bearing witness in response to the witness. It becomes a question of truthfulness.

The Bible testifies to the self-disclosure of God. Its ways of speaking are responses to God's presence and absence, and how that has been known. They are testimonies of the memory and anticipation of the God known in many and various ways. They are the trace in language of the mystery, and they bear within them, they *embody* the dynamic of that knowing. Knowing is relationship. The loss of ways of knowing is the loss of ways of being in relationship. It is the loss of relationship with the God who is known differently in parable, hymn, lament, law, wisdom, myth, history — and for that matter, in preaching. Whoever God is and shall be for us, and however else it pleases God to be made known to us, the path of interpretation leads to the holy city by way of these beautiful gates, each one a pearl, each a pearl of great price.

Five

Voice and Witness

"The voice comes before the sign, but is it not from the start the voice of the sign?"
                                                                    —Jabès[1]

And there was evening and there was morning. It is not yet the Lord's Day, and not yet the Day of the Lord. Still, salvation is nearer than it was, and the day at hand is for doing the work for which you have been sent, while you can.
                                                    —Romans 13:12, John 9:4

"Thank you for coming," she said. She gestured toward a chair beside the daybed where she sat propped up by pillows. "You may turn on the light if it helps you see."

"I'm Jeanette's pastor. She..."

"Yes, I know. Jeanette worries about me. She needn't, but she does."

"She thought there might be something you'd want to talk about."

"Well, she worries, as I said. But I'm past worry, long past. I have no questions, and I am not afraid." She offered a half-smile,

157

reassurance that she meant her words kindly. "And there's not much pain. That's a blessing."

She looked around the room slowly, as if the vases, pictures, and little boxes needed reassurance, too. At last her gaze fell upon the nightstand and the Bible there. With two hands she lifted it onto her lap and opened it at the book-mark. She pressed down the pages with a smoothing motion then laid the fingers of her right hand beneath the words at the top of the page. She read slowly and precisely, "The Gospel According to Saint John." Without looking up, "This has always been my favorite. I used to be able to recite so much of it from memory. I may have been a little too proud of that, because the words seem to have left me. And now when I try to read I can only make out the big letters on the page, like 'The Gospel According to Saint John.' "

Her fingertips caressed the page lightly. She didn't speak for several moments. "There *is* something you could do," she said at last, looking up. "I hesitate to ask, because it would take quite a little time. And despite Jeanette, we're still strangers."

"What would you like me to do?"

She looked back at the page, "I would love to hear the Gospel According to Saint John. I'd love to hear it read aloud. If you have the time."

What other answer could you give? "Yes, I have the time. I'm free the rest of the afternoon."

"Read," she said, "like you're reading to someone hearing it for the last time. Can you do that?"

"I can try."

"Well, when you stumble, dear, I'll help you say the words. I'll say them as they come back to me. We'll do it together." She handed over the Bible. "Thank you."

"I will need to pray a little while before beginning."

"Yes."

"The Gospel According to Saint John. In the beginning was the Word: the Word was with God and the Word was God...."

And finally, much later: "This disciple is the one who testifies to these things and has written them down, and we know that his testimony is true. There were many other things that Jesus did: if all were written down, the world itself, I suppose, would not hold all the books that would have to be written."

Voice

The scriptures upon your desk are silent, and the silence is a gift. Despite the longing, and even the prayer that the scriptures speak, this they cannot (and must not) do if they are to be the scriptures. And I must understand that if I am to enter into relationship with them *as* scripture this silence is necessary. It is through this silence that they fulfill their vocation.

The voice dies in writing, and must die if it is to inherit the future. And the writing is raised into a new voice, a new body, a different glory, through reading and speaking. Whatever the voice was, it has been transformed into writing, and is a voice no longer. It can never become again the voice it was. The only way to keep faith with the writing's past is by its transformation. Keeping faith with what is written does not rest with repetition. We keep faith through the transformation of what is written into new speech. If the scriptures lead beyond themselves, it will be because they have been received first of all *as* themselves. If they lead to a voice, if someone speaks, it will have to be in a voice that is really a voice.

Today it is the scripture that is being read, and read for a reason: to become voice once more, a voice now. Voice is often a metaphor for self, person, identity. To have a voice means to have power, a standpoint, authority, something to say. Voice discloses the one from whom it comes, and brings forward from within what cannot be seen. It carries, therefore, the sense of both hiding and revealing. Voice represents the one who speaks, so that to listen to, or ignore, or disobey the voice means to do so to the one who has spoken.[2] But it is not only to others that a voice reveals the speaker. My voice discloses me to myself as well.

Voice is not only a metaphor for identity, however. It is first of all my actual speaking aloud. If voice is a powerful metaphor in the ways we have indicated, then it is exactly because my actual speaking aloud discloses so much. At the start, therefore, if *I* am to read, read as myself, it is not enough to read silently. Your voice forces you to make choices that your eyes do not. Your voice can never be empty of meaning, or let us say intention, that is, *how* you mean. Try to speak like a machine, and you communicate mechanism. Try to speak without inflection and you communicate a fear to speak. We have no alternative. Just as our bodies are always enacting something — even if it is immobility and rigidity — our voices are always expressing meaning, intention.

Listen to your own speaking, then, to hear what it tells you. The words on the page carry vast possibilities of meaning, oceans are there. Yet as one of my teachers insisted, "To have a hundred choices is not freedom; it is in choosing that you are free." And how will we know what we have chosen until we have heard for ourselves what is there to be said?

Maurice Blanchot wrote,

> The reading of a poem is the poem itself.... It is the poem giving birth, in the space held open by the reader, to the reading that welcomes it; it is the poem become power to read, becoming communication opened.... To read is thus not to obtain communication through the work, but to "make" the work communicate itself.[3]

Although Blanchot refers to a poem, there is no reason to restrict his insight to the poem alone, as he himself does not. Let us claim that what he says of a poem is true of scripture as well, maybe even more true if one believes that scripture is for the sake of preaching. Do you believe that what was written in former days was written for our sakes? Written so that we might speak to one another, welcome one another as we have been welcomed? Written so that what was once promised and heard by our ancestors in faith might be heard again by the nations? Written so that it might be heard so clearly that we and they knew (at last) that it was for us together and be filled with hope (this is Paul's insistence in Romans 15)? One who believes that scripture is for the sake of preaching might indeed press Blanchot's claim even further.

Return to Blanchot, substitute the word "scripture" for the word "poem," and you will have a foundational statement of the relationship between scripture and reading. And if what he says is true of one person reading alone, and silently, how much more true is it of one who reads aloud? Scripture is not the marks on the page, for scripture that is not read is not scripture. That is why, when the lost book of the law had been found and read aloud, Josiah tore his clothes and sent to Huldah the prophet to know what it all meant (2 Kings 22). That is why Nehemiah assembled all the people before the Water Gate and the law was read with interpretation so the people could understand, for which reason Ezra said, "This day is holy to the LORD your God" (Neh. 8:9). That is why Jesus said, "Today this scripture is fulfilled in your hearing," for it is by hearing that scripture is fulfilled. Scripture happens in the reading of the scripture.

Here is the paradox: for the voice to be saved it must be lost as a voice.[4] In place of the lost voice is the writing, and nothing can restore the voice behind the writing. If there is to be a voice again it cannot be the same voice; it must be a new voice. "Unless a grain of wheat falls into the earth and dies...." "The one who would save her life will lose it; the one who loses her life for my sake and the gospel will save it."

"How are the dead raised? With what kind of body do they come?" (1 Cor. 15:35). Paul gives a strange and beautiful answer. He speaks of birds, fish, heavenly and earthly bodies, sun, moon, stars, and glory. Resurrection is transformation. It really is the death of the body, and must be. And it really is the resurrection of the body, he declares, or we are most to be pitied. But it is not the resuscitation of a dead past; keeping faith with the past does not mean its repetition. It is, instead, a transformation into the image of what comes from the other direction to meet us: the same one who went before, in the way of death and transformation and was made new, as all things are promised to be made.

Death and resurrection as an image of writing and reading? An imperfect image, of course, and we are not God, one hastens to add, to resurrect what has been written. But perhaps it can help us to glimpse what is at stake in the interpretation of writing for speaking. For we who await the transformation of heaven and earth — who groan with anticipation, as Paul has it — keeping faith with what is written does not rest with repetition. We keep faith through the transformation of what is written into new speech.

If the voice is to be saved it has to be lost into writing, we have said. The writing, in its turn, awaits transformation as well. Although we have spoken of writing's transformation into new voice as a resurrection, this resurrection is also loss. As writing awaiting new voice the possibilities are open. As writing newly voiced, the possibilities are set aside for *this* voice, *this* speaking, *your* voice, *your* speaking. Even the resurrection of the body, if it is true to the life of the body, takes *place*. If resurrection includes taking a real place then it includes this loss: the loss of possibilities in order once more and newly to become real.

I had occasion once to read aloud a passage from Jonathan Kozol's *Amazing Grace*.[5] A twelve-year-old boy named Anthony had written about "God's Kingdom" as he imagined it from his neighborhood in the South Bronx, New York. He imagined the street people there, friendly animals, no television, the prophets, no guns or drugs, and other transformations of the world surrounding him. I had read the words many times and thought about what they meant and how they meant. The words I was reading aloud were all familiar words to me, and there was nothing there that should surprise me. Then I came to these sentences: "You'll recognize all the children who have died when they were little. Jesus will be good to them and play with them. At night he'll come and visit at your house. God will be fond of you." What took me completely unprepared was my own voice. My voice recognized more clearly than I did that these words could not just be read. My voice simply stopped, and I couldn't speak. Not *didn't* speak, but *couldn't* speak. No sounds would come from my mouth until at last I began to shake, and finally to weep. When my eyes no longer could see the words on the page (words I knew by heart), haltingly, almost one at a time, my voice then pronounced them.

I tell this both reluctantly and with amazement. Such things happen, as it happened once to Paul on the Damascus road where his eyes became useless to him, and his own voice and his ears transformed the road itself into a place of conversion. Such things can and may happen when the interpreter is taken by surprise in the open, in the in-between where even your own voice is both not your own and most your own. For the in-between is the place where you are required to testify and to hear your own testimony. In the in-between you are a witness to your own witness, and as with everyone who hears a witness, you must decide and choose for or against what you hear.

Turn on the radio to listen to the preachers whose voices can be heard only late at night and at the edges of the dial. Some nights what you will hear is a kind of duet. A preacher calls out "Read" and another voice answers, reading the scripture. After every verse the preacher repeats what has been read, but with a different voicing — different feeling, different tone, to a different purpose. Finally, the preacher calls out "Stop!" and begins to repeat one verse over and over, the same words each time, but each reading different, and the people answer back to show they hear the difference. Speaking and listening at the same time, the preacher clears a resonant space for discovering what the words say, a resonant time for exploring publicly in the way that only a voice can.

Explanation and understanding

Voice forces you to make choices, or to reveal the choices you have made, we have said. The language of choice can be deceiving, however, because it suggests issues that are primarily rational or willful. Let us say instead that voice reveals *relationship*.

Literary critics distinguish between sense, feeling, tone, and intention in interpretation.[6] "Sense" means the semantic meaning of a text. "God is coming" is a simple declarative sentence, clear enough as a sentence (although not clear at all in what it might mean). "Feeling" refers to the speaker's emotional relationship to that sense. For example, one can say "God is coming" with joy, fear, anticipation, or apprehension. This may be the best news or the worst news, but what kind of news the speaker finds it to be can come to expression only through the voice. "Tone" refers to the speaker's emotional relationship to the audience. I may, indeed, find the news to be appalling but at the same time acknowledge through my voice that for you the news is wonderful. Or I may say the same words with the wag of a taunting finger that promises the listeners are about to *get it* at last as they so richly deserve. "Intention" refers to the particular combination of sense, feeling, and tone. Why this sense with this feeling and this tone? Although it may sound complicated to describe, our speech communicates in this way all the time. This is not virtuosity, but the kind of ordinary talk one hears on any bus or at any kitchen table. Or perhaps it is a kind of virtuosity, the kind that possesses the speaker when we forget about speaking and are given over to speaking itself: not a strategy but a way of being in relationship.

The expression of meaning then becomes inseparable from the appropriation of meaning on the part of the interpreter. Relationship will be expressed, and the voice will interpret. To give voice to the text, simply to read it aloud situates the reader, and not always as the reader would necessarily choose to be situated. It is a broadly shared insight that reading aloud is the first level of interpretation.[7] It presents the "fore-understanding" or projection of meaning that begins the interpretive dialogue. All the subsequent methods that seek to discover the possibilities for being proposed by the world of the text lead to a new voicing that presents the text, the reader, and the hearer in their relationship.

This is the famous hermeneutical dialectic of explanation and understanding. What is at stake in the distinction is how the so-called objective and subjective moments can be held together. Explanatory methods are those critical, formal approaches to a text that serve to bracket (at least provisionally) the self-understanding of the interpreter. (This returns us to our consideration of self-understanding as both a barrier and a bridge.) The various kinds of critical method offer possibilities for discerning patterns and meanings in the texts that my own self-interest clouds or obscures. One deploys tools of literary, historical, cultural, political, economic, or theological analysis and examines the text with their help. By providing critical distance, these methods are deployed against the silencing or distorting power of tradition and inherited reading, a power that works most effectively when it is unrecognized. Whether or not critical methods actually work that way, of course, is a matter of intense debate.[8]

The dimension of understanding "precedes, accompanies, closes, and thus *envelops* explanation. In return, explanation *develops* understanding analytically" (Ricoeur).[9] That is, self-understanding is the starting place of interpretation, but it must be temporarily bracketed by explanatory methods. If those brackets are left in place, however, interpretation remains distant from the text's demands and possibilities as real demands and possibilities for our own lives. The brackets must be removed, therefore, and the demands and possibilities taken to ourselves, or appropriated. This does not mean that they are necessarily accepted, but it does mean that they confront our self-understanding. In the face of these possibilities for meaning and action in my world, my self-understanding is disclosed, and either confirmed or transformed. It may be that I take up these possibilities into my own life; it may be that I reject them. But in either case, my self-understanding is now an understanding "before" or "in front of" the text.

Response and responsibility

In this sense, understanding means *response*. Understanding is demonstrated, enacted in life. The question of the relationship between explanation and understanding is sometimes named as the question of method versus truth. "Method," in this sense, is the critical, formal, distanced approach to the text. "Truth," by contrast, means participation, belonging, the "fusion of horizons" whereby the interpreter is affected by an experience of historical understanding. So much of preparation for ministry is training in the method of reading the scriptures. In Bible courses we learn to read as discerning textual critics. Theology courses help us understand how to work with the Bible theologically and what a theology *about* the Bible might be. Courses in cultural and social criticism help us understand the contexts and forces at work within both the world of the Bible and our own communities. That was not what a dying woman was asking for, however. She was not listening for my expertise in method and analysis; she was listening to hear if there was truth in my voice that spoke to the truth of that culminating time of her life.

What happens when we move from understandings of validity that are tied to the dimension of explanation (with its values of unitary or univocal reading), which is inevitably reductive, toward an understanding of validity that is *expansive*, that is, an understanding of validity that corresponds to the excess, the more, the multiple possibilities of the text, to which no singular interpreter is adequate? As Levinas says, the infinity of the text (not the totality) requires a plurality of interpreters "in their uniqueness, each one capable of wresting meanings from the signs, each time inimitable."

> It all happens as though the multiplicity of persons . . . were the condition for the fullness of "absolute truth," as though each person, through his [or her] uniqueness, ensured the revelation of a unique aspect of the truth, and that certain sides of it would never reveal themselves if certain people were missing from [humankind].[10]

If certain people were missing from humankind: what a haunting phrase to evoke our need for one another in the work of interpretation. When I read aloud "Do not let your hearts be troubled. Believe in God, believe also in me" (John 14:1), I knew how to read as a young man seeking to comfort an aged woman approaching her death. I did not know how to read as an aged woman who knew these words by heart and believed them, and *trusted* herself to them. She had to teach me in the only way she could: by saying the words herself so I could hear the unique aspect of the truth she knew that day.

If certain people were missing from humankind: the simple fact, of course, is that certain people go missing from humankind every day and their loss confronts us with God's anguished question to Cain: Where is your brother? Where is your sister? Their loss confronts us with the question of how our own ways of interpreting are implicated. When we understand validity of interpretation to include the dimension of response in the realm of self-understanding and action, the "test" of validity becomes that of ethical response before the "absolute claim of the other" (Levinas).

Take, as an example, Judges 11:29–40, the story of Jephthah's daughter (one of the texts of terror, as Phyllis Trible so powerfully named them). Jephthah had made a vow to God promising that if he were given victory against the Ammonites he would make a burnt offering of whoever first came out of his house to meet him at his return. It was his daughter, his only child, who came out dancing to greet him. He granted her two months to lament with her companions, then "did with her according to the vow he had made." Every year, therefore, "the daughters of Israel would go out to lament the daughter of Jephthah the Gileadite" (Judg. 11:39–40). What must valid interpretation of the story of Jephthah's daughter include? At the level of text-centered explanatory interpretation there need not be a response. It is sufficient to account for the various dimensions of the text, whether literary, historical, cultural, political, sexual, theological, or religious. One can comment upon the meaning of sacrifice (animal and human), let's say, or the force of a vow, the relationship between Israelites and Canaanites and how it affected worship in Israel, or one can consider the pathos and tragedy of the story and its characters. When the question of validity in *response and responsibility* is posed, however, then another kind of enquiry must take place. How are the lives of women and girls disposed, disposed of, and destroyed (both figuratively and literally) by the actions of men? Where do women and girls suffer this destruction in our own communities? How is this permitted or even justified by our scriptures and the ways we read them? Interpretation that continues on this path cannot rest in commentary, but will have to take the form of recognition, horror, repentance, and resistance.

Augustine wrote his treatise *On the Spirit and the Letter* in 412 CE, eleven or so years after the completion of the *Confessions*. It is an anti-Pelagian work devoted in the main to Augustine's understanding of the working of grace. Although the argument is one of doctrine, the treatise begins with and is founded upon problems of interpretation theory.

As the title indicates, the question of the relationship between letter and spirit is the subject matter, but Augustine makes a different kind of argument. In *On Christian Doctrine* the letter was to the spirit as the literal was to the figurative. The goal of interpretation was to pass beyond the letter to the spirit, and indeed, failure to do so was a kind of carnality. Spirit stood in opposition to literalism, whether it be naïve, mistaken, or perverse. Spirit was fulfillment, completion. Spirit represented a higher knowledge, a deeper wisdom in the rule of faith and charity. Yet in *On the Spirit and the Letter,* Augustine admits that the chief meaning of Paul's words, "the letter kills but the spirit gives life," does not have to do with figurative expressions versus literal ones. It has to do with the power to live rightly.[11] Founding his argument on his reading of Romans, Augustine says the letter tells us what we must do, but the spirit empowers us to do it. Without the power to do what is good, the law only makes us aware of sin, either goading us toward it or reinforcing our sense of powerlessness in the face of it. The gospel brings more than information a person might receive and act upon. It is the effective Word, which by the power of Holy Spirit gives grace to respond in faith. Our sanctification is the effective work of this same Word by the power of the Spirit to write the law of love upon our hearts.

The problem of teaching and learning is still of concern, but learning is presented now in different terms than in *Of the Teacher* and *On Christian Doctrine*. There learning meant grasping the meaning of another, whether person, text, or God. Here it means the power to *do* that meaning, to do what is known to be right. The shift is not so much a change of position but a movement to deeper implications. That shift affects, in turn, the prior question of interpretation as we shall see in the conclusion of *On Christian Doctrine* (completed in 427 CE). The question could be put this way: how does the understanding of the nature of interpretation change if the goal is no longer the grasping of a meaning but a change of life?

This, of course, is a fundamental concern of the Protestant Reformation. On one hand, Luther (for example) was much more positive about the value of the literal or (so-called) historical reading of the scriptures. As with the interpreters of the school of Antioch — Theodore of Mopsuestia and John Chrysostom would be prime examples — or the sober precision of Aquinas, he found the plain sense preferable to elaborations of allegory. In this way he stood in tension hermeneutically (although not so much theologically) with Augustine. On another hand, Luther may be read as pressing the same issue. To understand the scripture for Luther means to understand how we stand before what it declares, to experience its meaning as a meaning for and about us, and to receive its transformative power.

> When I was a monk, I was an expert in allegories, I allegorized everything. Afterwards through the Epistle to the Romans I came to some knowledge of Christ. There I saw that allegories were not what Christ meant, but what Christ was.[12]

A distinction both delicate and bold. If the tradition of allegory pointed away from Christ, Luther wanted to reverse the direction. For his interpretation Christ would be the center, and Christ was what was to be understood. The interpretive center, as with Augustine, must be identified with a kind of principle (Christ), but also with the experience of being addressed and grasped in one's heart. Here is a characterization of Luther's hermeneutic by Gerald Bruns:

> Here the text is no so much an object of understanding as a component of it; what one understands when one understands the scriptural texts is not anything conceptual and extractable as a meaning. Rather, what one understands (that is, enters into) is the mode of being or life of faith informed by the text.[13]

To understand in this sense is to hear oneself addressed and to experience the very contradiction of letter and spirit as the reality of one's own situation. Luther's commentary on Psalm 119:125 even presses to say that the experience (or responsibility) of interpretation is essential, indeed irreplaceable. Because the received interpretation takes the place or substitutes for the encounter with the scripture itself it must be considered the dead letter from which one must depart. Validity in interpretation reaches beyond construing a text to construing a life.

When I was small, my grandmother's housekeeper would ask, "Do you *hear* me, boy?" Her question was not about my ears but my feet. Understanding, in her view, meant doing what she had told me to do. I have known the commandments of God since I was perhaps six years old, or at least known enough to be able to recite them. What I want very much to know is where the power comes from to enable me to do them.

Primitivity

So, remembering the words of the Preface, think of a preacher who is once again preparing to preach — not preparing a sermon, which is a noun, but preparing to preach, which is a verb, something you do. Think about a preacher who, for whatever reason (perhaps the grace of God!), hesitates. Before the book is opened, before there is a mark on the page, before there is a text in which to lose oneself, before the particularity of certain words and images, and the inevitable absorption into their own networks and connections, this preacher hesitates and asks, "What is it I am preparing to do?"

Think of the situation of a teacher of the church who is once again preparing to teach; not preparing a lecture, but to teach. Think about a teacher who, for whatever reason, hesitates: who tries to remember where teaching begins and why, who tries to remember what teaching is for and what it hopes, who tries to remember what it is to learn and how that has actually happened in the teacher's own life.

Think of a person sitting in a church pew on a Sunday morning who hesitates. Think of a person who in courage, let us say, or even forgetfulness or innocence asks, Why am I here? Is it because there is something I want to know? feel? hear? see? do? be? And if it actually happened would it really make all the difference?

Think of two friends sitting together at the table with the night opening up ahead of them. Two longtime friends sit together, calm in a way, and uneasy in a way, because they know there is nothing they may not say to one another. There is nothing to hide, nothing so important or trivial that it lies outside the bounds. They may speak of their heart-most desires or the sale in the paper. They are friends, but what is it friendship does? Now they hesitate. What will they say?

Think of two enemies who know that their enmity is destroying them and those they love. Think of them face to face searching for reconciliation and peace, searching for something that can happen both within them and between them that will make it possible. Something that is so difficult and so simple, so complex and so singular, so profoundly human and so profoundly particular to who they are, that they know what is at stake there is at stake everywhere, and what is at stake everywhere is at stake there where they meet. Or think about the family that will gather to make their momentous decision, or the congregation that will gather to make theirs.

These people share what Søren Kierkegaard might call "Primitivity," or "Naivete." It is an individual's own sense of his or her own life or existence or personhood, a sense of "I" that resists being absorbed into the ground of others' lives and languages, others' reasons and explanation, others' questions and answers, and insists upon a kind of truth that is authentic to the existence of the one who tells it (*Journals,* vol. 1, no. 654).[14] The words "primitivity" and "naivete" are by no means derogatory for Kierkegaard. To him these were qualities every life should have.

> Every existence ought to have primitivity. But the primitive existence always contains a reexamination of the fundamental. What is the significance of a primitive genius? It is not so much to produce something absolutely new, for there really is nothing new under the sun, as it is to reexamine the universally human, the fundamental question. This is honesty in the deepest sense. (*Journals,* vol. 1, no. 657)

Honesty, it would seem, has to do with thinking about the fundamental questions of a life. It also has to do, however, with asking how such questions lead a person beyond the terms of an individual life toward the life humankind shares. Honesty of this kind reaches to speak of human experience, not only one human's experience — a dangerous attempt, certainly, with many attendant possibilities for wrongdoing, too dangerous to be left in the hands of the few. Better for each person to share the task and the responsibility, better for each person to claim the right to think about life from where they live, in honesty. The task requires, paradoxically, such great power of concentration *and* great power of letting go. A single lived honesty is so costly it must be held fast, but it can be held fast honestly only if it is released again and again to relearn its truth.[15]

The people in these situations share such honesty, we could say, and this honesty takes the form of a question about what they are preparing to do. And because it is this peculiar kind of honesty, the question searches the paths of their own hearts as the path toward a human heart larger than their own.

However else we might name what each person is hoping for in such a situation, each could recognize at bottom a desire that communication happen. Whether by them or to them, through them, because of them, or in spite of them, it is a desire that there be communication. Call it a desire to have communicated what is most important, however it is named, because this is what they believe it means to be a preacher, a teacher, a worshiper, a friend, a peacemaker: to be in communication about what is most important.

This has such a modest — even naïve — sound to it: to be in communication about what is most important. The desire to communicate is easy enough to name; to name what is most important is much harder — not unlike, in the end, pronouncing the name of God. And to say how, if at all, such a thing can be communicated from one person to another! Where do you start? Where do you go? Where do you end?

It brings a person into the realm of fundamental questions: What is the reality of my own life? How can I speak about it? How can I tell the truth? What have I believed? *When* have I actually believed in ways that mattered? To what have I truly committed my life? How do I know? What do I hope? What does that hope look like when I live it? Why should anyone else listen to such things? What does my own life have to do with what is most important for someone else? To think about communicating with another person we are turned back to think about one's own life and how it stands before the life of another. Primitivity has a way of spreading out from its original question. To ask about one fundamental I have to ask about another, and on and on.

One word the Christian church has used in particular to name what is most important is "faith." It is to faithfulness that the preacher invites the congregation; it is toward faithfulness that the teacher guides the learner; it is for faithfulness that the parent hopes to equip the child; it is in search of faithfulness that the worshiper comes to pray; it is by faithfulness that friends are friends; it is through faithfulness that enemies can make peace.

There are other words, of course, by which we may come to speak of what matters most. Speak of hope, speak of love, speak of grace, speak of justice, speak of mercy — which one of them could be left out? Such words, in fact, need each other. If you begin with one of them to say what you mean, do you not find that you must turn to the others, and others beyond those?

By faith I do not mean to indicate one particularly excellent word over other excellent words, but to speak of what holds them together in their mutual difficulty and mutual necessity. To speak of faith, in this sense, is to speak of a kind of passion (this is Kierkegaard's word for it), because each of these most excellent words is full of paradox, and paradoxical with each other, as well. Each of them speaks to and from the places of sheerest tension: between the interior and the exterior, the personal and the communal, history and the moment, experience and ideal, belief and unbelief, time and eternity. That is what makes such words important: not that they rescue us from all this, but because they are themselves the difficult language of the in-between.

Faith, paradox, and passion

Faith, as Kierkegaard presented it, is paradox and passion. It is a paradox in the deepest sense; more than a contradiction, it is an absurdity. A harsh word "absurdity," but one with which Christian tradition is familiar. To call the paradox absurd is to say that there is a kind of offense in it. A paradox can be merely a curiosity, a matter of interest, but of no great importance. People seem to be able to hold two contradictory opinions at the same time without too much difficulty, as we see in *Alice through the Looking Glass*. But to hold a paradox with passion, to found one's life upon an unrelievable paradox is a different matter. Before the bar of reason it is more than wrong: it is utterly foolish.

To hold to such a paradox therefore means that one is far past being simply mistaken; one has become a fool. The person who holds to the absurd becomes absurd. The absurdity for Kierkegaard is this: "...that the eternal truth has come into being in time, that God has come into being, has been born...quite indistinguishable from other individual human beings" (*Postscript*, 188).[16]

This is the deepest absurdity imaginable in the world of Kierkegaard's thought, and this deepest absurdity remains steadfastly absurd. Its scandal cannot be resolved. It cannot be proven or established in any objective way, any historical way. It can never become a self-evident fact to which a person might reasonably subscribe, a thoughtful conclusion to well-presented evidence. "The characteristic mark of Christianity is the paradox, the absolute paradox" (*Postscript*, 480). It can be held only in faith. It is the object of faith that cannot be held objectively. It cannot be known; it can only be believed. The object of faith is the reality of God becoming a particular individual, existing as a particular individual, becoming the teacher (*Postscript*, 290). This teacher's reality can never be encompassed in the content of the teaching, at least in such a way that the teacher fades but the teaching endures. Therefore, "the maximum attainment within the sphere of faith is to become infinitely interested in the reality of the teacher" (*Postscript*, 291). And what became of this teacher? Suffering.

Infinite interest joins utter absurdity. The deepest inwardness holds to an object that can never be known. What is it that joins and holds together these great opposing paradoxical horses? The passion called faith. Moment by moment this is the task: to discover the paradox anew, and to hold together in the ordinary moment time and eternity, the finite and the infinite (*Postscript*, 207). This is the task: to believe in the very streets that run past one's door, in the unremarkable occupations of an hour, putting the possibility of this reality to every moment, however impossibly distant from such reality it may appear. As Kierkegaard wrote in one of his journals, "Faith is essentially this: to hold fast to possibility" (*Journals,* vol. 2, no. 1126). Passion, then, is the pull that holds possibility in the face of impossibility, of absurdity, of the ultimate paradox. Such passion both holds the two together and refuses any attempt to make them one. The paradox is not to be overcome, the incomprehensibility of it is not to be overcome; rather it is to be deepened and endured. Christianity " ... makes existence paradoxical and remains paradoxical as long as one exists, and only eternity possesses the explanation" (*Postscript,* 499). And the word that must be emphasized for Kierkegaard here is "existence." It is not simply thinking that is made paradoxical, a kind of dialectical gnosis by which one secretly comprehends all (*Postscript,* 496). Existence itself, in all its concreteness, is the place where one has to deal with eternity. Eternity in time, infinity in finitude. It is the very "repulsion" of the paradox, the impossibility of any such direct and unparadoxical grasp which draws one ever more deeply into a dynamic of passion. Faith holds this paradox and lives it in the utmost interior of one's life, from where all of one's life flows. Infinite absurdity requires infinite passion.

This work of infinite passion is not a work an observer can see. The picture of the person holding heaven and earth together in the deepest passion may be a picture of a woman sitting at her desk balancing the weekly budget. It may be a man sitting in the park feeding the birds. It may be two strangers talking together waiting for a train. There is no way to tell for sure, at least no way that can't be turned upside down into something else. For passion holds heaven and earth together only within a person, only for a moment, a moment which can't be seen. Then the work begins again (*Postscript,* 176). At most one might see the fruit of passion, as one can see the fruit of love.

It had happened like this, the summer before.

He pulled the van off the road and parked. A footpath led away down the slope through the woods to the river. As he followed it the sound of the road became fainter, and by the time he got to the riverbank, the sound of water over the rocks washed other noises away. The river wasn't very deep there, maybe knee-deep, and wide enough that the open sky stood overhead, filled with strong midday light.

He sat down, unlaced the work boots, and eased them off his feet. He removed his socks and stuffed them inside. He reached inside the bib pocket of his paint splattered coveralls for the little book that was there and then laid it aside on the ground. He pulled off the coveralls, then the T-shirt, placing them by the boots. Cut-offs would have to do. Close enough.

He stepped into the water gingerly, feeling for footing, the little book in his left hand. A big rock in midstream, the kind that trout like to hide behind, made a pocket in the current. He worked across the current until he stood in the still place behind the rock and faced upstream. He opened the little book, which had several pieces of torn paper stuck in its pages.

He read aloud, "Repent and be baptized every one of you in the name of Jesus Christ so that your sins may be forgiven; and you will receive the gift of Holy Spirit." Turning to a second marked passage he read, "Look, here is water! What is to prevent me from being baptized?"

Then holding the testament high in his left hand he went down on his knees in the stream. With his right hand cupped he poured handful after handful of water over his head repeating, "I repent, I repent, I repent...."

At last he stopped pouring and continued kneeling a while, still and in silence. He stood up, wiped his eyes, and looked up into the sky. The light was bright enough to hurt. Swallows dove and turned overhead. He listened closely: only the flight call of the swallows and the water over the rocks. Nothing more.

He turned once again to the testament and read aloud, "Do you not know that all of us who have been baptized into Christ Jesus were baptized into his death? Therefore we have been buried with him by baptism into death so that, just as Christ was raised from the dead by the glory of the Father, so we too might walk in newness of life."

He waded to shore and looked back out toward the eddy behind the rock, following with his eyes the course that the water took as it continued downstream.

That was how it had happened.

Communication

As Kierkegaard deeply confronted the problem of Christian life for himself, the problem of the preaching and teaching of the church became more urgent. How can one communicate something that has ultimately to do with profound inward transformation? How do you communicate what can be truly learned only in existence? How can you speak of the suffering of Christ without betraying it? Kierkegaard's famous attacks on the church of his time were rooted in convictions about how the Christian life and message were authentically communicated.

Christianity, he recognized, begins with something of which one must be told: the reality of Christ. While that remains an objective uncertainty held fast in passion, knowledge of that uncertainty is essential. The question of the communication of faith finally comes to focus upon two issues: how communication can involve "reduplication," and the nature of witness. Reduplication is Kierkegaard's term for a person's existential enacting or demonstration of what is said. "Preaching should have of all things the very closest relationship to existing" (*Journals*, vol. 1, no. 644). The truest form of communication is to show. Showing, however, is an indirect form of communication because it is living rather than speaking. Showing must be accompanied by saying. The indirect must be accompanied by the direct. Direct communication is not oration. If it is an art, it is the art of simplicity. The greatest simplicity, in fact, is that a person's life expresses what the words say; "to act is to make simple" (*Journals*, vol. 1, no. 663, no. 665).

This means that authentic preaching depends upon a setting in which Christian life is actually at stake. But since it is always and everywhere at stake (existence being what it is), that means a situation in which what is at stake in such speaking and hearing is made audible and visible.

Kierkegaard recorded in his journals a marvelous imaginary scene. A theologian labored for years to become famous so that people of all situations and ranks would flock to hear what the theologian preached. He puts out the announcement of an upcoming sermon at the finest church in the capital, and everyone comes, especially the rich and the royal, to hear such a renowned speaker. The text is the story of Jesus driving the money changers out of the temple.

He begins by declaring that all his life's work was in preparation for this declaration of the word. "To preach Christianity in these surroundings is not Christianity. . . . Christianity can only be preached in actual life. And I hereby transform this building into actuality. I am now in your power. . . . " The theologian then proceeds to declare the poverty and suffering of Christ in so direct a speech than the congregation becomes enraged and thunders against the preacher, to which he replies,

> " 'Now this is right; now I am preaching Christianity. If my intention had been suspected I would have been kept out of this pulpit or everyone would have stayed home. But here I stand and I am speaking, and I charge you in responsibility toward God to listen to me, for it is the truth which I speak.' "

This would be an awakening. (*Journals*, vol. 1, no. 667)

He doesn't say for *whom* it would be an awakening, however; perhaps for the preacher and congregation alike.

What Christian preaching so often misses, Kierkegaard believed, is the *situation*. Or better to say it this way: what it so often does is to evade the situation in which it takes place. It either avoids proclamation in the situation where what is at stake in Christianity is plain for all to see, or conspires with the congregation to make it invisible. What such communication lacks is the quality of *witness*.

Communication of what is Christian ends in witness. More than either form of communication, direct or indirect, it enacts the existential situation of Christian faith. Witness stands between the two. It is direct because it tells of Christ; it is indirect because it can show only the witness's life. It is direct because it names Christ's suffering and humiliation in contradiction; it is indirect because it can only invite the hearer to follow. It is direct because it points to the power of God; it is indirect because it can show only the weakness of the witness.

Witness, we might say, is the theater of faith. It is living person to living person, I to I. It is embedded, embodied, confessional, testimonial, fragile, incomplete, inevitably paradoxical, inevitably offensive. All of this is only to say that it is the enacting of the passion of faith. To hear is the same. It means to turn toward the scandal, offense, and contradiction scandalized, offended, crossed, because that is not the enemy of faith; it is the requirement of faith. As a hearer let me not congratulate myself that the preaching finds me unoffended; let me ask instead if perhaps that is because no gospel was preached, or I was too thick or too frightened to hear.

Authentic witness, then, becomes a double enacting of faith. The witness enacts the suffering and contradiction in what is said, the hearer in the appropriation of what is heard. In the end, it is a theater in which the hearer is the most important witness. It is the hearer who finally makes what happens into an existential communication of Christian life by taking it to the hearer's own life.[17]

The rhetoric of life

The conclusion of *On Christian Doctrine* waited more than thirty years to be completed, in 427 CE, only three years before Augustine's death. The writer was in his old age, but the age to which he belonged had grown old, too.[18] The classical world was in eclipse. The Vandals were at the door of the city. The stability of culture, easy assumptions of education, knowledge, the commerce of learning and ideas were no longer possible. Perhaps the decades of preaching had taken their toll, as well. Interpretation, for Augustine, had always been set squarely in the context of preaching to a Christian community; it had always been an interpretation *of* a text *for* a community. The pondering of divine mysteries has a way of giving over to the pondering of human mysteries when it is to the human mystery one must speak year after year.

The conclusion of the work, Book IV, brings us back to the problem of interpretation *for,* the problem of communication, teaching, preaching. What is most striking is the forked nature of the argument. Perhaps that is because Augustine himself was forked, aware of the powerful pulls within him. He was no stranger to contradiction, after all, and desires in conflict. If Christian life was inevitably struggle in the ambiguity of the world, it was equally a struggle within the Christian, or at least within *that* Christian. In the end, to which voice would the decision go? To the theologian, bishop, and rhetorician? Or to the preacher, the supplicant, the sinner whose own salvation must be worked out in fear and trembling? After all the years, books, fights, preaching, praying, what *wisdom* is there to share? The struggle may be seen mirrored in the unfolding of the text itself.

On one hand, Augustine moves toward a reduction of the value of rhetoric for teaching. On another hand, he admits the value of it for certain purposes, most importantly the purpose of persuading the hearer. But if the persuasion is not to come from the rhetorical skill of the preacher, from where is it to come? The argument flows back and forth through Book IV, only to find its surprising resolution in what might be called a *rhetoric of life.*

Having attended to how one discovers what is to be taught, it would be reasonable to expect a similar building up of the technique of preaching or teaching. That would be, indeed, a classical rhetorical movement itself. Having discovered, one arranges and delivers, and does so in accordance with certain insights that are both psychological and aesthetic. Eventually, he does just this, but his initial movement is in the opposite direction, a movement of subtraction rather than addition.

First comes an attack upon rhetorical method itself. Rhetoric is partial neither to true interpretation nor false, a longstanding critique familiar to the philosophical descendents of Plato and Aristotle. It is a technical form that is merely neutral in the question of truth. It is not to be shunned, but it must be treated cautiously. Even so, it is not something one can really *study* with any profit. Eloquence, he says, can be best learned by listening to the eloquent; those who are able to learn it will do so rather quickly, those unable will not benefit from any amount of instruction (*On Christian Doctrine* IV.1.2–IV.3.5). It becomes part of you or it doesn't, and if it does become part of you it operates, he argues, in a largely unconscious way. Study of the rules helps one to recognize eloquence but not to practice it.

The preacher/teacher is, in fact, caught in a dilemma, perhaps so great as to be called a paradox. One is called upon to teach what has been learned, to communicate wisdom. But Augustine has already acknowledged that speech can't really teach what is most important. At most it can direct the hearer toward the Internal Teacher. Words are the occasion for learning, but not the cause; they are a provocation of a search that can come to fruit only by the grace of God working within. If the real function (if not intention) of language is to direct a person's gaze within to God, if the real function of language is to move the hearer to seek the God who teaches and bestows grace, then rhetoric as the art of persuasion acquires a renewed purpose.

The scriptures themselves represent to Augustine the embodiment, the inscription of the reconciliation of wisdom and eloquence. The problem is that the eloquence of scripture belongs only to scripture. It is not to be imitated, only presented so that it can be heard. The aim of the Christian teacher, therefore, is clarity; the goal is to be understood (IV.8.22). Language that is simple and direct is the vehicle by which what is hidden is made visible (IV.11.26). When it is understood, however, the problem of persuasion remains. The understanding and the affections are not the same. There remains the realm of love, fear, hate, sorrow, joy, pity, and it is these, in Augustine's analysis, which move persons to do what they know (IV.12.27).

The orator must then delight and persuade the hearer as well as teach. To this end, Augustine allows, the insights of rhetoric have much to offer. Study Cicero, if you will; learn of the subdued, moderate, and grand styles if you can. Of greater help, however, is *prayer*. Because there is only one teacher who knows the hearts of all and knows how to speak to all, it is the inner speaking of Christ — not Cicero — which gives the proper eloquence.

Old habits die hard, however, and Augustine's argument turns once more to the opposite pole as he moves among the various combinations and possibilities of style: how effective this manner is for that purpose, how manners complement each other, how the speaker may achieve surprising ends with surprising means (IV.17.24–26.58). The discussion unfolds as the musing of an old orator who has promised not to lecture on rhetoric, but who has spoken of so much, so often, and to so many, that he writes about it in spite of himself. He has already insisted that the true eloquence of words is beyond the speaker's grasp; still, there is an undeniable delight he takes in the flesh of eloquence that could cause a reader to smile. Augustine's delight makes the conclusion to the work all the more poignant.

The young man sat at the table in the church study. He had appeared at the door during the lunch hour, asking for the minister. He had looked around uncertainly when invited into the study. The walls of books seemed to be both a source of amazement and amusement. "Have you read all these books?"

A common question. The answer is no. Some people have the sin of hoarding money, a kind of insurance against future need; preachers tend toward the sin of hoarding books, a different kind of insurance against a different kind of need. But it's not just hoarding. Some of those books are friends, and better friends than those you have coffee with. Still, the question is always a little embarrassing, or the answer is.

It was the story about the ten lepers that had stuck in his mind, he said. How Jesus had healed them, how nine of them never looked back. Maybe that was a good thing, he thought. If you had been a leper and suddenly were healed, maybe new life itself, living whole, was the most important thing. Did Jesus heal them so they'd be grateful? Or did he heal them so they'd be free? Free, he figured. Otherwise, Jesus was just like anybody else: give a favor to get a favor, build up chips to call in. A little guilt here, a little shame there, a little debt, just like anybody else. Let 'em go, God bless 'em. More power. Pay it along, not back, he thought.

"And that's fine for the nine, Reverend. I don't worry about them. But I'm number ten." His gaze was level and unblinking. "I'm number ten," he repeated, reaching into the bib of his coveralls and taking out a small pocket testament. "I'm the one who went back to Jesus to say thanks. In the Bible it says Jesus told the lepers to show themselves to a priest to prove that they were clean. That's what I'm doing."

"Showing me that you're clean?"

He held out his hand, fingers spread, palm down. "See that? Dead steady. Look at my eyes. What do you see?"

They seemed clear and focused, alive. "Your eyes look fine."

"That's right. Clean. Washed clean. In the river. By Jesus."

"I'd like to hear about it."

"Do you believe Jesus can still baptize someone?" he asked. "Or does some minister have to do it?"

"Well, there's a story in Acts about people being baptized with Holy Spirit first, and water second. And sometimes the water comes first and the Spirit second."

"Who baptized you, Reverend?"

"I don't know. I was a baby. It was my parents' minister."

Looking around the room at all the books, he nodded his head as if some idea he had was just confirmed. "Are all these books about God?"

"Most of them, one way or another."

Nodding still, he said again, "I'm number ten. I'm here because of Jesus. Jesus sent me to you, I guess you could say, like in the Bible."

"I'm glad you've come."

He looked around the room again, his eyes traveling across the shelves, weighing what he would say next.

Finally he spoke. "Here's my question, Reverend: When Jesus sent that leper to the priest, who was it for? Was it for the leper or was it for the priest?"

The witness and the trial

The end of *On Christian Doctrine* belongs to a different rhetoric, one we might call a *rhetoric of life*. What is the presentation of wisdom that teaches, delights, and moves? The presentation of a life, the speaker's own transformed life. Words serve wisdom, and wisdom serves the life obedient to Christ (IV.27.59–31.64). The life of charity itself is the text, the speech the Christian teacher must put before the congregation. The life of charity is the life transformed by the grace of God, the life that shows forth the cross of Christ (1 Cor. 1:17). What matters is presenting the truth, and truth is not finally a matter of rhetoric; it is a matter of life, but *life with words*. The teacher "*so acts with words* that the truth becomes clear, that the truth is pleasing, that the truth moves" (IV.28.61, emphasis added).

The purpose of teaching is still to instruct, please, and move; one still makes use of words. But see how the teacher and the words are turned to point beyond themselves. It is not the teacher's words that instruct, please, and move. It is not the preacher's life that instructs, pleases, and moves. It is the *truth* that does all of these, and the task of the preacher is to act in such a way, to join life and proclamation in such a way, that the truth itself will do what it is needed to do.

If one does not have the gift of eloquence, this is finally a small matter. If the words of others can help, let them help (although not by representing them as one's own). Falsehood and the theft of speech are not matters of repeating the words of others (for what do we have but what has been given?) — a perhaps surprising theological affirmation of the intertextuality of our speech. The real falsehood and the theft of words are in the disjunction of speech and life. Life and speech deconstruct one another, we might say now. Speech-signs and action-signs are regions of a common realm of truth, to be spoken together and read together. Let the preacher's life be so ordered that it is itself an eloquent speech (IV.29.61). This is witness.

In its small and flawed way, the life of charity is the earthly image of the heavenly text "read" by the angels, who read without syllables the face of God. For those who want to teach the truth and move others to embrace it with their own lives, the most important words are those of prayer, asking God to shape the speaker's life into a life that is true. And the hearers, let them pray in this way, too, for the preacher and themselves; for must they not also speak and act from what has been given them?

> Those also who are about to speak what has been delivered to them from others should pray for those from whom they receive it, before they receive it, that they may be given what they wish to receive. And when they have received it, they should pray that they may deliver it well, and that those to whom they offer it may take it; and for the profitable result of their speech they should give thanks to [the One] from whom they should not doubt they have received it, so that [one] who glories may glory in [the One] in whose "hand are both we and our words." (IV.XXX.63)

The language of witness and testimony is most familiar to us from the situation of a trial. This is a reality with which our usage of the language must come to terms. What is it that makes a trial? It is not the question of guilt or innocence but the question of truth, and the need to respond to the truth. The trial is hermeneutical, because in it the realms of fact, speech, and interpretation meet. Not only must they meet, there must be some decision, upon which individuals and the community will act. Some will testify. Others will argue. Others will listen and decide for or against. Still others will then act. The consequences may, indeed, be as grave as life and death. They may be much more ordinary, as well, and ordinarily are. But either way, the bond between life and speaking is completely exposed there (for good and ill), from the mundane to the most consequential. Acknowledged or not, our lives are always in the midst of such trials, exposed and vulnerable to what others say. Someone testifies, someone argues, others decide for or against, still others act. The commandment against bearing false witness must be heard in the café as well as the courtroom.

In a formal trial, however, there is an aspect of this that becomes visible with a clarity not usually found in the context of teaching or preaching: the situation of the one who must hear testimony. Testimony in this context goes far beyond the purpose of sharing one's perspective or view with those who may or may not have any need to respond. In a trial, testimony is addressed to those who must make a decision, who have accepted the responsibility to make a decision. Perhaps you have served on a trial jury, and held that responsibility. Perhaps you have had to announce a verdict, or even to sign your own name, attesting to what the jury has decided. Perhaps you know how a person's hand can shake when the time comes to do so.

A witness is a person who testifies in a dispute about the truth. A witness stands between the realm of action, of things seen and heard, and the realm of speech, things said. A witness also stands between the realm of things said and the realm of things believed and acted upon. Thus, she stands between action and action. A witness stands at the place where not only a particular aspect of truth is contested, but where also is contested the possibility of truth itself.[19]

So in a dispute about the truth a witness is summoned to testify. By testifying a witness does more than simply express an opinion. A witness makes an outward attestation of an inward conviction, indeed, an inward faith. What a witness testifies to, however, is something known in the visible and tangible life of the world. Conviction or faith is inward, but their risk is that they make a claim about something true in the world we share. Integrity is the binding together of this inward and outward dimension, and integrity is what makes a true witness. One may ultimately be mistaken, outweighed by the testimony of other witnesses or rejected, and still not be a false witness, for the integrity of the witness does not depend upon the outcome of the trial. It is not being mistaken, outweighed, or rejected that makes one a false witness; it is the lie. "False testimony is a lie in the heart of the witness."[20]

We have spoken of the lie before, and now once again. The lie in the heart is first of all a lie to oneself. The question of truth also, then, is posed first of all within the witness. The witness must first confront the witness's own testimony with the question of truth, and within him or herself claim the responsibility of "I." Like the prophet, although perhaps even more nakedly, the witness stands in the place of the truth to which the witness testifies.

Testimony cannot give us truth itself, but only a witness to the truth. "Testimony *gives* something to be interpreted" (Ricoeur).[21] It presents the "crisis of appearances" whereby one must decide between true and false witness.[22] The only way one can decide is by entering this crisis of appearances, entering the in-between of event and meaning, because there is no other way to become responsible. There is no other way, because testimony itself places the hearer where the hearer must choose and take responsibility.

What emerges more and more as the question of interpretation of testimony unfolds is this position of the hearer, the one who must decide. From the focus upon the nature of event, witness, attestation, and testimony the spotlight turns emphatically toward those to whom testimony is presented. If it is first of all because of what one has witnessed that one testifies, it is, finally, for the sake of those others who must understand and act that one testifies. A witness testifies, but it is the verdict of those who must decide that is carried out.

There is, indeed, a trial underway in the world; it is, indeed, a dispute about the truth. If your ears have been opened, if you have been given the tongue of someone who has been taught, if you have learned (however imperfectly) how to sustain the weary with a word, you have already appeared in the trial. You know what it means to be confronted by adversaries. You know the strange experience of appearing as a witness only to be accused and convicted yourself. You would also know, I hope, what it means to have the vindicator as your helper.

Impossible possibility

Who could presume to present himself or herself as living speech? Who would dare to say their life embodies the proclamation of the gospel? Who would claim to be telling the truth? This would be the gravest, the most impossible responsibility. Yet who would deny that whether one dares it or not, whether we choose it or not, for good and for ill, that is what we do?

> As ministers we ought to speak of God. We are human, however, and so cannot speak of God. We ought, there-fore, to recognize both our obligation and our inability and by that very recognition give God the glory. This is our perplexity. The rest of our task fades into insignificance in comparison.[23]

The impossibility is not different for ministers than for anyone else. Whether anyone actually notices this is a different matter. But the paradox of obligation and inability is "simply" the para-dox of the way things are. At one moment it is the preacher who is caught out in it; at another moment it is the three friends at the table; at another moment it is the strangers on the bus. There may be a difference of the degree of exposure, of course. The min-ister is exposed to, by, and in this impossibility so publicly that it may enter into the minister's awareness more resonantly. The task of preaching confronts the minister with the contradiction, discloses the minister by the minister's response, and displays it before others when the community gathers, so that our failure (which is less serious than our seeming success) is there for all to see. The only question is what one will do in the face of infinite obligation and the small powers of *response-ability* we command. Self-deception (whether of power or weakness)? Hubris? Despair?

Mystification? Absorption in the mundane? Avoidance? Any and all of these are real choices, perhaps the most realistic choices. Any and all of these are, even more realistically, the natural way to drift. It is probably the slow movement of the tide that takes us, as much as setting a course away from the in-between, which if it is a still place, is so only in the passionate contradiction of self-awareness and self-forgetfulness. It is the situation of anyone who would bear witness to the truth.

It is, in fact, the special responsibility of the preacher to *call attention* to the shared contradiction and impossibility for the sake of hearer and speaker alike. It is the special responsibility of the preacher to speak in such a way that it is clear that one is at most a witness. More modestly, it may even be that one is a witness to the witness of others: witness to a witness to a witness.

Nevertheless (a word to which we keep returning) this contradiction and impossibility do not dismiss, excuse, or exclude the preacher. Quite the opposite. In the face of the impossibility one need neither pretend nor apologize. One must tell the truth as a witness. Ultimately, our forms of preaching, our models for sermonizing, our techniques of interpretation are indifferent to what is essential. They can be empty or full, good or bad, more clever or less, more complex or more simple; they can become forms of responsibility or irresponsibility, either one. The most crucial question for the preacher is how, in this way or that, one takes responsibility before the face of the other in, by, and through what one says.

This is to say, one is *free* to tell the truth as a witness regardless of the folly and weakness. It is, indeed, our very inability that is required, because it pleases God by the folly of what we preach, to save. One is *so* free, in fact, that the freedom has this quality of an imperative. I must, not because I am required to, but because I *may,* and I *can.* That is why the place where one gives glory to God is in the middle: in between.

A portion of Augustine's sermon on Psalm 32 gives a picture of the end of such glory.[24] The text is, "Rejoice in the Lord, O ye just. Give praise to the Lord on the harp; sing to [God] with the psaltery, the instrument of ten strings. Sing to [God] a new canticle. Sing well to [God]."

Augustine's lyrical response suffers in paraphrase, but the meaning is clear, even in a more simple prose. It is the one born of grace who can sing the new song, he says. Life is the language for singing it, not words. But who would dare sing for such an implacable listener as God? What kind of life sings beautifully to so perfect a critic? The life that sings the very tune God gives, he answers, a tune of jubilation. Jubilation signifies nothing but the end of signs. "Words cannot communicate the song of the heart." As workers in the midst of their difficult work begin to sing with words, they come to leave words behind, "and break into the free melody of pure jubilation." It makes no difference that it cannot be understood, because this is speech past understanding. It is not about joy; it is joy. It is not about God; it is the telling *of* God. This, too, is witness. Witness beyond witness.

The simple and the difficult

It begins in the morning. The tongue of one who is taught. Method and discipline. The spiritual. Spiritual discipline. In the beginning — Brooding over the face of the deep. The contradiction of contradiction. Knowledge. Fortitude. The counsel of mercy. Love of the enemy. Wisdom.

The life of interpretation. The middle. Inwardness. Relationship. Thou. Situation. Embodiment. Totality, Infinity, and the Face. Self-understanding.

In the middle of language. Speaking a world. Breaking the bonds of deadly words. The preparation of freedom. Re-membering. The poesis of life. From the mystery of language to the language of mystery. The mystery of God. Word and God. God and truth. To believe the Word. Listening for the Word.

The Book. Writing, not speaking. Scripture and sacredness. Revelation. Ways of knowing. A storied world. Knowing by doing. Call, re-calling, re-membering, standing in the place of truth. Speaking in parables. Wisdom. Hymning and healing. Gates to the city.

Voice. Explanation and understanding. Response and responsibility. Primitivity. Faith, paradox, and passion. Communication. The rhetoric of life. The witness and the trial. Impossible possibility. The simple and the difficult.

These are aspects of the life of interpretation, the life of preaching. The mystery of each one goes far beyond anything we have been able to say. And all these together are not enough to do more than gesture toward what interpretation presents us in any ordinary day. It is not through these that we finally enter into the mystery of interpretation, but the other way around. The common task of interpretation opens out into this broad land, flowing with milk and honey.

How many days has it been now? Is it time already to preach again?

What is asked of you is simple; therefore what is asked of you is difficult. Gather the people, break the bread, tell the story. Do justice, love mercy, walk humbly. Ask, seek, knock. Most simple, most difficult.

As simple as slipping into the water, as simple as sitting down at the table. As simple as making a promise. As difficult as keeping a promise. As difficult as doing what is right. As difficult as saying yes, saying no, saying stop, saying come.

It is so simple and difficult that it is all mystery. That's what mystery is. Not puzzlement and obfuscation, but the place where the simple and the difficult meet. And each place they meet is a different mystery. The mystery of the stranger at the table is one, but the mystery of the friend by your side is another. The mystery of giving is one, but the mystery of receiving is another. The mystery of listening is one, but the mystery of speaking is another. And, and, and...and the cup of cold water, and the candle on the table, and the book that's in your hand, and the skin upon your hand, and the color of your skin, and how you are a woman and how you are a man. Mystery upon mystery, grace upon grace. Grace so poured out into the world, there is nowhere else to look. Gather the people, break the bread, tell the story. Do justice, love mercy, walk humbly. Ask, seek, knock.

"Think of us," Paul writes, "as stewards of the mysteries of God" (Gather the people, break the bread, tell the story). "As good stewards of the manifold grace of God, serve one another with whatever gift each of you has received" (1 Pet. 4:10). (Do justice, love mercy, walk humbly.) "Confess your sins to one another, and pray for one another, so that you may be healed" (James 5:16) (Ask, seek, knock).

And you, too, are a mystery of God, worthy of stewardship.

Most gracious God: Speak to me that I may speak. Give me, I pray, the tongue of one who is taught, that I may sustain and be sustained. In the trial, strengthen me to give true witness. Walk with me in the holy darkness where your name is heard. Receive me at the last. Raise me up with all the others in the final victory of life over death, when all things are made new. Then, I pray, once again speak to me, that I may speak.

Notes

One: In the Beginning

1. Cited in Harold Stahmer, *"Speak That I May See Thee"*: *The Religious Significance of Language* (New York: Macmillan, 1968), 113.

2. Henri de Lubac, *Medieval Exegesis: The Four Senses of Scripture* (Grand Rapids, Mich.: Wm. B. Eerdmans, 1998), 1:17, 19, n. 71.

3. Bernard McGinn, *The Growth of Mysticism: Gregory the Great through the 12th Century* (New York: Crossroad Herder, 1996), 81.

4. Augustine, *On Christian Doctrine,* trans. D. W. Robertson (New York: Liberal Arts Press, 1958), II.7.9.

Two: A Life of Interpretation

1. Rainer Maria Rilke, *The Notebooks of Malte Laurids Brigge,* trans. Stephen Mitchell (New York: Vintage, 1985), 19–20. See W. Dow Edgerton, "Ways of Praise," *Theology Today* 43, no. 4 (January 1987): 472–86, for a treatment of Rilke and the vocation of poetry.

2. Søren Kierkegaard, *Søren Kierkegaard's Journals and Papers,* ed. and trans. Howard V. Hong and Edna H. Hong (Bloomington: Indiana University Press, 1967), no. 644. Hereafter cited as *Journals.*

3. Søren Kierkegaard, *Concluding Unscientific Postscript,* trans. David F. Swenson and Walter L. Lowrie (Princeton, N.J.: Princeton University Press, 1968), 177. Hereafter cited as *Postscript.*

4. Søren Kierkegaard, *Works of Love: Some Christian Reflections in the Form of Discourses,* trans. Howard and Edna Hong (New York: Harper & Row, 1962), 28.

5. Ibid., 26–28.

6. The term "I-Thou" may be found earlier in the work of Feuerbach. Others developing the theological or philosophical understanding of relationality include Ferdinand Ebner, Franz Rosenzweig, and Eugene Rosenstock-Huessy. See Shmuel Hugo Bergman, *Dialogical Philosophy from Kierkegaard to Buber* (Albany: SUNY Press, 1991); Harold Stahmer, *"Speak That I May See Thee!": The Religious Significance of Language* (New York: Macmillan, 1968); Martin Buber, *I and Thou,* 2nd ed., trans. Ronald Gregor Smith (New York: Charles Scribner's Sons, 1958); "The History of the Dialogical Principle," afterword by Martin Buber in Buber, *Between Man and Man* (New York: Routledge & Kegan Paul, 1947). The question of the mutual influence of Ebner and Buber seems largely agreed as coincidence, although some journal publications may

show thematic similarities. Ebner was reluctant to recognize affinities between his work, Rosenzweig's, and Buber's (or Feuerbach's, for that matter), and came to appreciation of the connections only later. See Rivka Horowitz, "Buber and Ebner: Intellectual Cross-Fertilization between a Catholic and a Jew," *Judaism* 32 (Spring 1983): 188–95.

7. Maurice S. Friedman, *Martin Buber: The Life of Dialogue* (New York: Harper & Row, 1955), 34f.

8. For a close analysis of Buber's *I and Thou* see Robert E. Wood, *Martin Buber's Ontology* (Evanston, Ill.: Northwestern University Press, 1969).

9. Martin Buber, *Knowledge of Man*, ed. Maurice Friedman, trans. Maurice Friedman and Ronald Gregor Smith (New York: Harper & Bros., 1964), 81.

10. Buber, *Between Man and Man*, 14.

11. George Eliot, *Middlemarch*, ed. W. J. Harvey (New York: Penguin, 1965), 226.

12. Gabriel Marcel, in *The Philosophy of Martin Buber*, ed. Paul Schlipp and Maurice Friedman, Library of Living Philosophers 12 (LaSalle, Ill.: Open Court Press, 1991), 46.

13. Gabriel Marcel, *Being and Having*, trans. Katharine Farrer (Boston: Beacon Press, 1951), 10.

14. Erwin W. Straus and Michael A. Machado, "Gabriel Marcel's Notion of Incarnate Being," in *The Philosophy of Gabriel Marcel*, ed. Paul Arthur Schlipp and Lewis Edwin Hahn, Library of Living Philosophers 17 (LaSalle, Ill.: Open Court Press), 137.

15. Ibid., 121–55.

16. Emmanuel Levinas, "Martin Buber, Gabriel Marcel, and Philosophy," Haim Gordon and Jochanan Bloch, eds., *Martin Buber, A Centenary Volume* (New York: Ktav, 1984), 309.

17. Emmanuel Levinas, *Outside the Subject,* trans. Michael B. Smith (Stanford, Calif.: Stanford University Press, 1994), 35.

18. Levinas, as cited in Jill Robbins, *Prodigal Son/Elder Brother: Interpretation and Alterity in Augustine, Petrach, Kafka, Levinas* (Chicago: University of Chicago Press, 1991), 142. Original citation in Emmanuel Levinas, *Totality and Infinity: An Essay on Exteriority,* trans. Alphonsos Lingus (Pittsburgh: Duquesne University Press, 1969), 199.

19. Levinas, as cited in Robbins, *Prodigal Son,* 142.

20. Levinas, *Totality and Infinity*, 213, cited in Robbins, *Prodigal Son,* 144.

21. Levinas, *Outside the Subject,* 44.

22. Levinas, "Kierkegaard: Existence and Ethics," in Emmanuel Levinas, *Proper Names,* trans. Michael B. Smith (Stanford, Calif.: Stanford University Press, 1996), 74.

23. See Paul Ricoeur, *Interpretation Theory: Discourse and the Surplus of Meaning* (Fort Worth: Texas Christian University Press, 1976).

Three: The Mystery of Language

1. The names commonly associated with the perspectives here would include Wittgenstein, Heidegger, various descendants of Saussure, Merleau-Ponty, Ebeling, and Ricoeur. Gerhard Ebeling's *Introduction to a Theological Theory of Language* (Philadelphia: Fortress Press, 1971), Robert Funk's *Language, Hermeneutic, and Word of God* (New York: Harper & Row, 1966), and Theodore Jennings's *Beyond Theism* (New York: Oxford University Press, 1985) are particularly helpful explorations of the linguistic themes in their application to theology. Rebecca Chopp's *The Power to Speak: Feminism, Language, God* (New York: Crossroad, 1989) works through issues of linguisticality and liberation in dialogue especially with French and American post-structuralist feminism. I have found her work extremely stimulating and helpful in articulating my understanding of the Word of God.

2. As Heidegger observes, "We always see the nature of language only to the extent to which language itself has us in view, has appropriated us to itself." See Martin Heidegger, "The Way to Language," in *On the Way to Language* (New York: Harper & Row, 1971), 134.

3. Joseph Margolis, "Phenomenology and Metaphysics: Husserl, Heidegger, and Merleau-Ponty," in *Merleau-Ponty Vivant*, ed. M. C. Dillon (Albany: SUNY Press, 1991), 153.

4. Rainer Maria Rilke, "The Ninth Elegy," from *Duino Elegies*, in *The Selected Poems of Rainer Maria Rilke*, trans. Stephen Mitchell (New York: Vintage Books, 1984), 199f.

5. Heidegger talks of Being as "hailing" and drawing out our responding hail. For a very sympathetic and rather moving discussion of this in relation to poetry see Nathan A. Scott Jr., *The Poetics of Belief* (Chapel Hill: University of North Carolina Press, 1985), 146–68.

6. Augustine, *Confessions*, trans. Rex Warner (New York: Penguin Books, 1963), Book I, vi.

7. This is the great theme of Ernst Becker's *The Denial of Death* (New York: Free Press, 1973).

8. Aristotle, *Poetics*, IX. 1–3, in *Critical Theory since Plato*, ed. Hazard Adams (New York: Harcourt Brace Jovanovich, 1971), 53.

9. Gaston Bachelard, *The Poetics of Space*, trans. Marie Jolas (Boston: Beacon Press, 1969), xxiii.

10. Ibid., xix.

11. Cited in Robert Bly, "What the Image Can Do," in *Claims for Poetry*, ed. Donald Hall (Ann Arbor: University of Michigan Press, 1982), 42.

12. Bachelard, *The Poetics of Space*, xix.

13. Robert Bly, "A Wrong Turning in American Poetry," in *Claims for Poetry*, ed. Hall, 36.

14. Adrienne Rich, "Transcendental Etude," in *Dream of a Common Language: Poems 1974–1977* (New York: Norton, 1978).

15. Bachelard, *The Poetics of Space*, xxiii.

16. Margaret Atwood, *True Stories* (New York: Simon & Schuster, 1981), 67, 70.

17. Audre Lorde, "Poems Are Not Luxuries" in *Claims for Poetry,* ed. Hall, 283.

18. Philip Wheelwright, *The Burning Fountain: A Study in the Language of Symbolism* (Bloomington: Indiana University Press, 1954), 8–16. See also Nathan Scott's use of Wheelwright in *The Poetics of Belief.*

19. For a discussion of Hermes see W. Dow Edgerton, *The Passion of Interpretation,* Literary Currents in Biblical Interpretation (Louisville: Westminster John Knox Press, 1992), 18–42.

20. For an in-depth discussion of the problem of flux in experience as a hermeneutic issue see John D. Caputo, *Repetition, Deconstruction, and the Hermeneutic Project* (Bloomington: Indiana University Press, 1987).

21. Maria Rilke, "The Way In," *The Selected Poems of Rainer Maria Rilke,* trans. Robert Bly (New York: Harper & Row, 1981), 71. Used by permission.

22. A more distanced discussion might draw upon Merleau-Ponty's depiction of a "field of perception" and the relationship of foreground and background/ horizon. Rilke seems to image it much more vividly in just a few lines.

23. For a discussion of Rilke and the vocation of poetry see W. Dow Edgerton, "Ways of Praise," *Theology Today* 43, no. 4 (January 1987): 472–86.

24. The theme of drama or theater as a primary metaphor for the human situation is Marcelian, too, but would be common to other existential perspectives. See Paul Ricoeur, "Gabriel Marcel and Phenomenology," in *The Philosophy of Gabriel Marcel,* ed. Paul Arthur Schlipp and Lewis Edwin Hahn (LaSalle, Ill.: Open Court, 1984).

25. Gerald Bruns, *Hermeneutics Ancient and Modern* (New Haven: Yale University Press, 1992), 12.

26. David Tracy, *The Analogical Imagination: Christian Theology and the Culture of Pluralism* (New York: Crossroad, 1981), 163ff. This discussion is founded upon Tracy's analysis of the interpretation of the religious classic. Because of the way his analysis incorporates the basic hermeneutical approach of Paul Ricoeur, it is especially helpful here. As will be seen, Ricoeur's proposals concerning questions of revelation and genre are central to our path here ("Whole" must be approached with discernment, however, or at least with some clarification. It can be used in such a way that it communicates the very totalization away from which we have been pointing. It can be read as a synonym for the "One," which is not my sense at all.)

27. This is the sense in which Jacques Derrida may be understood to speak. For a highly nuanced discussion of this see John D. Caputo, *The Prayers and Tears of Jacques Derrida: Religion without Religion* (Bloomington: Indiana University Press, 1997), and *God, the Gift, and Postmodernism,* ed. John D. Caputo and Michael Scanlon (Bloomington: Indiana University Press, 1999).

28. Paul Ricoeur, *Figuring the Sacred: Religion, Narrative, and Imagination* (Minneapolis: Fortress Press, 1995), 225.

29. Ibid., 246. See also H. Richard Niebuhr, *The Meaning of Revelation* (New York: Macmillan, 1941).

30. Gerhard Ebeling, "The New Testament and the Hermeneutical Problem," in *The New Hermeneutic,* ed. James M. Robinson and John B. Cobb Jr. (New York: Harper & Row, 1964).

31. This is a phrase of Bonhoeffer's from a catechism he prepared for working with street youths in Berlin.

32. These are convictions which in some ways may be called philosophical, and their ancestry can be traced in various generations through such thinkers as Kierkegaard, Nietzsche, Dilthey, Marcel, Merleau-Ponty, Heidegger, and Ricoeur. They may also be met in a range of current critical perspectives, particularly those exploring dimensions of race, class, and gender and ways they contribute to how we experience ourselves in the world. But these convictions are also, and most important for the matter at hand, theological.

33. Gerhard Ebeling, "The Word of God and Hermeneutics," in *Word and Faith* (Philadelphia: Fortress Press, 1963), 305–32.

34. Gerhard Ebeling, *God and Word* (Philadelphia: Fortress Press, 1967), 2.

35. Ibid., 11.

36. This part of the discussion depends upon Theodore W. Jennings Jr., *Beyond Theism: A Grammar of God-Language* (New York: Oxford University Press, 1985), esp. 43–136.

37. Ibid., 122–23.

38. Ebeling, *Word and Faith*, 324.

39. Gerhard Ebeling, *The Nature of Faith,* trans. R. Gregor Smith (Philadelphia: Fortress Press, 1961), 82.

40. Ibid., 82.

41. For etymologies see *The Oxford English Dictionary* (Oxford: Oxford University Press, 1971).

42. See Ebeling, *The Nature of Faith*.

43. See Paul Ricoeur, "Toward a Hermeneutic of the Idea of Revelation," in *Essays in Biblical Interpretation,* ed. Lewis S. Mudge (Philadelphia: Fortress Press, 1980), 74. This focus upon what he calls the more originary expressions or confession of faith is taken up more specifically in following chapters.

44. Luther, commentary on Psalm 119:125, cited in Gerhard Ebeling, *Luther: An Introduction to His Thought,* trans. R. A. Wilson (Philadelphia: Fortress Press, 1972), 100.

45. Ibid., 99.

Four: Scripture as Scripture

1. Edmond Jabès, *The Book of Dialogue,* trans. Rosemarie Waldrop (Middletown, Conn.: Wesleyan University Press, 1987), 26.

2. Edmond Jabès, *The Book of Shares,* trans. Rosemarie Waldrop (Chicago: University of Chicago Press, 1989), 44.

3. Edmond Jabès, *The Book of Questions,* trans. Rosemarie Waldrop (Middletown, Conn.: Wesleyan University Press, 1972), 20.

4. Parts of this section appear also in W. Dow Edgerton, ed., *The Honeycomb of the Word: Essays in Honor of Andre Lacocque* (Chicago: Exploration Press, 2001).

5. Walter Ong, *Orality and Literacy: The Technologizing of the Word* (London and New York: Methuen, 1982).

6. Paul Ricoeur, "The Hermeneutical Function of Distanciation," in *Hermeneutics and the Human Sciences: Essays on Language, Action, and Interpretation,* ed. and trans. John B. Thompson (Cambridge: Cambridge University Press, 1981).

7. See W. Dow Edgerton, *The Passion of Interpretation,* Literary Currents in Biblical Interpretation (Louisville: Westminster John Knox Press, 1992), chap. 3.

8. For a discussion of Augustine's general theory of signs, see R. A. Marcus, "St. Augustine on Signs," *Phronesis* 2 (1957): 66–83. For his understanding of the difficulty of speech, see *On the Teacher,* and for scripture interpretation, *On Christian Doctrine.*

9. Paul Ricoeur, *Figuring the Sacred: Religion, Narrative, and Imagination* (Minneapolis: Fortress Press, 1995), 72.

10. Emmanuel Levinas, *Nine Talmudic Readings,* trans. Annette Aronowicz (Bloomington: University of Indiana Press, 1990), 8.

11. For a helpful historical discussion framing a constructive proposal see Ronald F. Thiemann, *Revelation and Theology: The Gospel as Narrated Promise* (Notre Dame, Ind.: University of Notre Dame Press, 1985).

12. See Avery Dulles, *Models of Revelation* (Maryknoll, N.Y.: Orbis Books, 1992); Ronald Thiemann, *Revelation and Theology* (Notre Dame, Ind.: University of Notre Dame Press, 1985).

13. Paul Ricoeur, "Toward a Hermeneutic of the Idea of Revelation" in *Essays in Biblical Interpretation,* ed. Lewis S. Mudge (Philadelphia: Fortress Press, 1980), 73.

14. Ricoeur, *Figuring the Sacred,* 224.

15. Paul Ricoeur, the essays "Toward a Hermeneutic of the Idea of Revelation," 73–118, and "Naming God" (*Figuring the Sacred*), are the key resources upon which this discussion rests.

16. Ricoeur, "Naming God."

17. Adele Berlin, *Poetics and Biblical Interpretation* (Sheffield, U.K.: Almond Press, 1983), 11.

18. See Robert Alter, *The Art of Biblical Narrative* (New York: Basic Books, 1981); Adele Berlin, *Poetics and Interpretation of Biblical Narrative* (Sheffield, U.K.: Almond Press, 1983); David Damrosch, *The Narrative Covenant: Transformation of Genre in the Growth of Biblical Literature* (San Francisco: Harper & Row, 1987); Ronald Thiemann, *Revelation and Theology: The Gospel of Narrative Promise* (Notre Dame, Ind.: University of Notre Dame Press, 1985), etc.

19. A foundational discussion of the "world of the text" can be found in Paul Ricoeur, *Interpretation Theory: Discourse and the Surplus of Meaning* (Fort Worth: Texas Christian University Press, 1976).

20. The work of Walter Brueggemann comes to mind as a particularly passionate advocate of the "strange world of the Bible (Barth)." As only one example see "The Third World of Evangelical Imagination," in Walter Brueggemann, *Interpretation and Obedience: Faithful Reading and Faithful Living* (Minneapolis: Fortress Press, 1991).

21. Jacques Derrida, *The Gift of Death,* trans. David Wills (Chicago: University of Chicago Press, 1996), 5–6.

22. Ricoeur's treatment of the "summoned subject" is my starting point here. See Paul Ricoeur, "The Summoned Subject in the School of the Narratives of the Prophetic Vocation," in *Figuring the Sacred,* 262–75.

23. Ricoeur, *Figuring the Sacred,* 266.

24. In my judgment, Abraham Heschel's treatment of prophetic passion and pathos is still most compelling. See Abraham J. Heschel, *The Prophets,* 2 vols. (New York: Harper & Row, 1962).

25. Stephen L. Wailes, *Medieval Allegories of Jesus' Parables* (Berkeley: University of California Press, 1987), 100.

26. See Bernard Brandon Scott, *Hear Then the Parable: A Commentary on the Parables of Jesus* (Minneapolis: Fortress Press, 1989), 7–63. William R. Herzog II, *Parables as Subversive Speech: Jesus as Pedagogue of the Oppressed* (Louisville: Westminster/John Knox, 1984), 7–30. John R. Donohue, *The Gospel in Parable: Metaphor, Narrative, and Theology in the Synoptic Gospels* (Minneapolis: Fortress Press, 1988), 1–28. John Dominic Crossan, *In Parables: The Challenge of the Historical Jesus* (Sonoma, Calif.: Polebridge Press, 1992), 1–37.

27. See Herzog, *Parables as Subversive Speech,* 13–15.

28. See Paul Ricoeur, *The Symbolism of Evil* (Boston: Beacon Press, 1967), 163.

29. Herzog, *Parables as Subversive Speech,* 47. See John Dominic Crossan, *The Dark Interval: Toward a Theology of Story* (Niles, Ill.: Argus Communications, 1975).

30. Scott, *Hear Then the Parable,* 48.

31. Ibid., 48.

32. Ricoeur, *Figuring the Sacred,* 149.

33. See Edgerton, *The Passion of Interpretation,* 115–38.

34. Scott, *Hear Then the Parable,* 62.

35. Ricoeur, *Essays in Biblical Interpretation,* 86.

36. Ibid., 86.

37. Ibid., 89.

38. Ricoeur, *Figuring the Sacred,* 227.

39. *Athanasius — The Life of Antony and The Letter to Marcellinus,* trans. and introduction by Robert C. Gregg, preface by William A. Clebsch, Classics of Western Spirituality (Mahwah, N.J.: Paulist Press, 1980).

40. For a discussion of the status of the text see M. J. Rondeau, "L'Epître à Marcellinus sur les Psaumes," *Vigiliae Christianae: Review of Early Christian Life and Language,* no. 22 (1968): 176–97.

41. For ease of reference, citations to the letter will be included in the text. The numbers indicate the paragraph of the letter, not the page numbers of the particular edition.

42. Frederick J. Ruf, "The Consequences of Genre: Narrative, Lyric, and Dramatic Intelligibility," *Journal of the American Academy of Religion* 62, no. 3 (1994): 799–818.

43. Ibid., 809.

44. Ibid., 815.

Five: Voice and Witness

1. Edmond Jabès, *The Book of Dialogue,* trans. Rosemarie Waldrop (Middletown, Conn.: Wesleyan University Press, 1987), 28.

2. For an influential discussion of the psycho-dynamics of orality see Walter J. Ong, *Orality and Literacy: The Technologizing of the Word* (London and New York: Methuen, 1982), 31–77.

3. Maurice Blanchot, *The Space of Literature,* trans. Ann Smock (Lincoln: University of Nebraska Press, 1982), 198.

4. This is what Ricoeur refers to when he observes that decontextualization, including the loss of the situation of address, is necessary for speech to be preserved as meaning, that is, writing. See Paul Ricoeur, *Interpretation Theory: Discourse and the Surplus of Meaning* (Fort Worth: Texas Christian University Press, 1976).

5. Jonathan Kozol, *Amazing Grace: The Lives of Children and the Conscience of a Nation* (New York: Crown Publishers, 1995), 237f.

6. See I. A. Richards, *Practical Criticism: A Study in Literary Judgment* (New York: Harcourt, Brace, & World, 1929), 173–81.

7. Richard Palmer, *Hermeneutics: Interpretation Theory in Schleiermacher, Dilthey, Heidegger, and Gadamer* (Evanston, Ill.: Northwestern University Press), 16–18.

8. Although participants in the debate are many, it is commonly named by reference to Hans-Georg Gadamer and Jürgen Habermas. Ricoeur's work approaches the question as a dialectical problem that brings explanation and understanding into mutual confrontation.

9. Paul Ricoeur, "Explanation and Understanding," in *The Philosophy of Paul Ricoeur: An Anthology of His Work,* ed. Charles E. Reagan and David Stewart (Boston: Beacon Press, 1978), 165.

10. Emmanuel Levinas, *Nine Talmudic Readings,* trans. Annette Aronowicz (Bloomington: University of Indiana Press, 1990), xvi.

11. Augustine, *On the Spirit and the Letter,* trans. W. J. Sparrow Simpson (London: SPCK, 1925), 6–9.

12. In Robert M. Grant with David Tracy, *A Short History of the Interpretation of the Bible,* 2nd ed. (Minneapolis: Fortress Press, 1984), 94.

13. Gerald Bruns, *Hermeneutics Ancient and Modern* (New Haven: Yale University Press, 1992), 145.

14. Citations from the journals are taken from *Søren Kierkegaard's Journals and Papers,* ed. and trans. Howard V. Hong and Edna H. Hong, 4 vols. (Bloomington: Indiana University Press, 1967), cited as *Journals.* Numbers refer to numbered entries and will be included in the text for ease of reference.

15. W. Dow Edgerton, *The Passion of Interpretation,* Literary Currents in Biblical Interpretation (Louisville: Westminster John Knox Press, 1992), 140.

16. Søren Kierkegaard, *Concluding Unscientific Postscript,* trans. David F. Swenson and Walter L. Lowrie (Princeton, N.J.: Princeton University Press, 1968). Cited as *Postscript.* For ease of reference, citations will appear in the body of the text.

17. Søren Kierkegaard, *Purity of Heart Is to Will One Thing: Spiritual Preparation for the Office of Confession,* trans. Douglas V. Steere (New York: Harper & Row, 1956), 180.

18. For historical background material see Peter Brown, *Augustine of Hippo* (Berkeley: University of California Press, 1967), 408–67.

19. Paul Ricoeur, "The Hermeneutics of Testimony," in *Essays in Biblical Interpretation,* ed. Lewis S. Mudge (Philadelphia: Fortress Press, 1980), 119–54.

20. Ibid., 128.

21. Ibid., 144.

22. Ibid., 144–46.

23. Karl Barth, *The Word of God and the Word of Man,* trans. Douglas Horton (New York: Harper, 1957), 186.

24. Augustine, *St. Augustine On the Psalms,* vol. 2, Ancient Christian Writers 30 (New York: Newman Press, 1961), 113–14.